UPSIDE DOWN

UPSIDE DOWN

HOW THE LEFT TURNED RIGHT INTO WRONG, TRUTH INTO LIES, AND GOOD INTO BAD

MARK DAVIS

REGNERY PUBLISHING

A Division of Salem Media Group

Regnery® is a registered trademark of Salem Communications Holding Corporation

Cataloging-in-Publication data on file with the Library of Congress

ISBN 978-1-62157-498-9

Published in the United States by
Regnery Publishing
A Division of Salem Media Group
300 New Jersey Ave NW
Washington, DC 20001
www.Regnery.com

Manufactured in the United States of America

10 9 8 7 6 5 4 3 2 1

Books are available in quantity for promotional or premium use. For information on discounts and terms, please visit our website: www.Regnery.com.

Distributed to the trade by
Perseus Distribution
250 West 57th Street
New York, NY 10107

To the leaders—in government, in churches, in communities, and in our families—who have the power to solve every problem in this book

CONTENTS

INTRODUCTION

I've always been a sucker for time-travel stories. As a kid, I would watch the deliciously cheesy *Time Tunnel*, a late-sixties Irwin Allen production featuring two scientists bouncing randomly through history, even though they always seemed to arrive at a place and time providing maximum drama, such as Hawaii the day before the Pearl Harbor attacks or the deck of the *Titanic* right before it hit the iceberg.

I have often thought someone should reverse that premise, writing stories of time-hoppers from the past leaping to the present day, just to see what they thought of how things are going.

Some of the reactions would be a joy to behold: the Wright brothers seeing mankind routinely in space, Hippocrates observing modern medicine, a slave witnessing our first African American president.

Other journeys might not go so well. One wonders what our Founders would think of First Amendment protections for pornography. A short time-jump by Dr. Martin Luther King would find him pleased with our racial progress yet heartbroken that so many of the grandchildren of the "I Have a Dream" generation are killing each other, and the occasional policeman.

No one needs to go back to our nation's birth, or even to our parents' birth, to imagine what would stun visitors from the past. Dazzling progress has been a constant theme in the history of America and the world, with new generations enjoying technologies and social changes unimagined just a few decades before.

But as the saying goes, not all change is progress.

The world of 2016 is an astonishing place. The America of 2016 is a wondrous creation. But both are mightily screwed up, in a long list of ways. The societal glue that has held us together is weakening, and some of our bonds have been willfully ripped apart.

Without a panel of time-traveling ancestors to weigh in on our errant paths, we are left to figure out solutions for ourselves. This is complicated because plenty of people around America and around the world think things are going just great. So what are the options for the rest of us, who see parts of the globe going mad, the foundations of our nation eroding, and the institutions that made America great falling into disfavor?

For a disease to grow into an epidemic, not *everyone* has to be infected. Likewise, folly and debased standards do not have to infect everyone, just enough to elect leaders who will govern us into the ditches of our own digging. Our troubled education system and our poisoned culture have corroded countless minds, mostly young. Some of them grow older and smarter but not all, leaving enough grown-ups to steer us very badly.

Policies, attitudes, even our own history—we should expect debates about all of these. We used to conduct those debates according to a shared set of rules, with a common understanding of who we are, what our nation stands for, what right and wrong mean, the basic concepts of man and woman, the value of God, the attributes of thoughtfulness and restraint. But so many givens have been swept away that healing our country and righting the world begin to look impossible. Faced with the daunting task of repairing so many things, where is the best place to begin?

To return to the medical metaphor, the first step is to diagnose the problem. Evaluate what seems to be out of whack, then see what needs to be done to correct it. The correcting part will require a long partnership between citizens, politicians, educators, clergy, soldiers, activists, and a universe of people in innumerable walks of life who see a suffering nation and a crazy world and want to make them better.

After more than thirty years of hosting talk shows and writing, usually addressing one problem at a time in a radio segment or column, I decided to produce a handy, book-length guide to the many ways in which the world is upside down. I consider a different issue in each chapter, posing several statements of the "conventional wisdom"—things you hear every day in the media or the classroom, from politicians and pundits, perhaps at church or in the carpool line—and offering a rejoinder to each.

Many folks who weigh in on society's manifold flaws can't resist scolding, and who wants to listen to that? If you're suggesting big changes, you need clarity, but you also need an upbeat message. More people will follow a happy warrior than a prophet of doom. Yes, we have a ton of problems. But my goal is to figure out how we got here and suggest solutions that actually attract people.

My prescription for our ills may appear to be a strong dose of conservatism, and that is precisely the point. You rarely hear the Left complaining that our nation and the world are adrift. Sure, some things draw their attention—incomes are unequal, there is still such a thing as the coal industry, and we don't have nearly enough transgender bathrooms, for starters. But in this second decade of the twenty-first century, liberals can look around and nod with satisfaction that things are going pretty much their way. They see a culture that they have shaped, a court system that does their bidding, bureaucracies that enforce their will, universities that fill young minds with their precepts, and a president who has pushed their agenda with a vengeance. If that's how we got here, maybe it's time to chart a new course.

Some of my prescriptions will be political, but not all. Many of our problems are not failures of politics but are crises of faith or acquiescence to the unfortunate elements of human nature.

No one is looking to re-create the past. Revisiting the "good old days" should make us appreciate how many things are better today. But we need to evaluate the thoughts and habits that have led us down some ruinous trails and see what we can change.

This is not the America we grew up in. But it's the America our kids are going to have to grow up in, and it's up to us to fix what we can, while we can.

1

HISTORY

The Founding Fathers are overrated.

These are tough times for the reputations of our nation's architects. Cynical journalists and academics treat the Founding Fathers
like relics of the dark ages, even villains, rather than visionaries who
laid the foundations of our freedom.

When did the flavor of American history change in our public
schools? My parents, teenagers in the 1940s, were taught about the
courage of the settlers, the sacrifices of the colonists, and the genius
of the very concept of America, a beacon for liberty around the world.
By the time I was swimming through adolescence, in the late 1960s
and early 1970s, we still caught glimpses of that America, but slavery
was becoming a consuming theme of U.S. history classes, and Vietnam dominated the headlines.

Any rendition of U.S. history must address slavery, obviously, but I recall hearing more about the horrors of slave auctions than about the courage of the millions of Americans who fought for emancipation. It did not occur to me when I was twelve, but our schools were being infected with the historical fallacy of viewing the past solely through the lens of our own sensibilities.

Seen through that lens, Columbus is not a courageous trailblazer who made the miracle of our nation possible. He is a European devil who victimized the indigenous peoples he found upon his arrival. For their execrable slaveholding and failure to extend voting rights to all, the Founding Fathers are the targets of similar derision from the ungrateful inheritors of the greatest nation in history.

No one suggests American history is free of blemishes. But our children and, far more oppressively, our college students are taught that our nation deserves some long overdue comeuppance. Our universities host departments whose purpose is to define America as racist and misogynist, placing the blame on the attitudes of the heroes who launched us on our journey.

Today's political battles are often between those who interpret the Constitution as originally written and those who wish to reshape it according to their preferences. If the Constitution is the product of exceptional genius, then the case for disregarding the intent of its designers is more difficult to make. But if it is nothing more than the handiwork of long-dead oppressors—the One Percent of the eighteenth century—then the Framers' opinions are more dismissible.

True, the Founders did not unite around an agenda of equality for all races or for women. This makes them seem fatally unenlightened against the backdrop of our century, where criticizing a black president draws catcalls of racism and opposing abortion is a "war on women." But if the passage of time is supposed to bring wisdom, it is worth noting that we have tossed aside some of the prudent judgments of 240 years ago in favor of the twaddle of current political correctness and faddism.

The minds beneath those powdered wigs devised a federal system that maximized freedom by keeping government authority as close to the people as possible while guaranteeing the rights of free expression, worship, and self-defense. Washington, Jefferson, Franklin, Madison, and their peers had no concept of a government so overweening that it would lure citizens into a lifetime of dependency on it. They knew immigrants would strengthen the new nation, but they would never have imagined a debate over whether the new arrivals should obey American law. They could not have foreseen the federal government's attempt to vitiate the "right of the people to keep and bear arms" that they enshrined in the Bill of Rights.

The Founders of the United States of America did not have twenty-first-century sensibilities about race, sex, or anything else. But neither did anyone else in the late eighteenth century. Our country has made enormous strides toward a more just society, some of them at the cost of an inconceivably bloody civil war. But we have made some serious missteps as well, blithely discarding the political wisdom of one of the most remarkable generations of statesmen the world has ever seen. We are not nearly as smart as we think we are.

The Constitution should change with the times.

President Barack Obama's successor might appoint as many as four justices to the U.S. Supreme Court. The 2016 presidential election will probably shape the court for decades.

The confirmation battles that gave us the Court of 2016 date back to President Ronald Reagan's nomination in 1986 of Antonin Scalia, who became the Court's longest-serving "textualist," his preferred term, indicating a habit of ruling based on the actual words of the Constitution, when possible.

A year later, the retirement of Nixon appointee Lewis Powell left a vacancy that Reagan chose to fill with Robert Bork, a legal giant slandered so viciously, and successfully, by his opponents that his surname became a verb, found in today's *Oxford English Dictionary*: "to defame or vilify (a person) systematically, esp. in the mass media, usually with the aim of preventing his or her appointment to public office."

And what earned Bork this torment? His embrace of originalism, the view that a judge should be bound by the inspired intentions of those who framed, proposed, and ratified the Constitution. As he explained, "The truth is that the judge who looks outside the Constitution always looks inside himself and nowhere else."[1] Such discipline is the enemy of the robed tyrants who twist the Constitution to fit their social aims.

Senator Edward M. Kennedy's attack on Bork is the stuff of dark legend. Faced with the prospect of a Reagan-appointed justice issuing rulings through the lens of the Framers' wisdom, the "Lion of the Senate" extended his claws and shredded the reputation of a brilliant jurist:

> Robert Bork's America is a land in which women would be forced into back-alley abortions, blacks would sit at segregated lunch counters, rogue police could break down citizens' doors in midnight raids, schoolchildren could not be taught about evolution, writers and artists could be censored at the whim of the Government, and the doors of the Federal courts would be shut on the fingers of millions of citizens for whom the judiciary is—and is often the

only—protector of the individual rights that are the heart of our democracy.

The world has changed since the adoption of our Constitution, to put it mildly, and we face questions about its meaning today that the Framers could never have anticipated. Does freedom of speech include dirty movies on cable television? Does the Fourth Amendment forbid NSA surveillance in a post-9/11 world? But such questions should be addressed within the constitutional framework erected in that Philadelphia summer of 1787. If that framework has become inadequate in some respect, it can be amended—by the people, not their judges. The alternative is an endless judicial rollercoaster ride. That's no way to run a legal system.

For all the headlines involving freedom of speech and religion (First Amendment), gun rights (Second Amendment), and government snooping (Fourth Amendment), the most pernicious threats to the Bill of Rights today concern the Ninth and Tenth Amendments. These two amendments guard something at the heart of our distinctive federalist system—the prerogatives of citizens acting through their states.

A Frenchman in Marseilles lives under the same umbrella of laws as his countrymen in Paris. An Englishman who moves from Leeds to London changes his address but not his legal system. But if you move from Alabama to California, or from Massachusetts to Utah, changes abound, and not just of culture and topography. Laws pertaining to countless layers of our individual and communal lives vary from state to state. Our Constitution respects and protects this glorious variety. These matters run far deeper than speed limits or the requirements for a law license. The definition of marriage and the regulation of abortion—nowhere mentioned in the federal

Constitution—are within the purview of our primordial governments, the states.

The Ninth Amendment provides that "the enumeration in the Constitution, of certain rights, shall not be construed to deny or disparage others retained by the people." In other words, no one should presume that rights not explicitly mentioned in the Constitution cannot naturally fall to the citizen. The Tenth Amendment reads, "The powers not delegated to the United States by the Constitution, nor prohibited by it to the States, are reserved to the States respectively, or to the people." In other words, matters that the Framers did not address are left to us to settle. Like same-sex marriage and abortion.

The problem is that many Americans seek to define some things as basic rights simply because they feel strongly about them, and they have found plenty of judges to help them. This is how decisions about abortion, "marriage equality," and now the protocols of public restrooms were snatched from the states, where citizens could properly debate how they wished to live. There's nothing wrong with a patchwork quilt of policies that reflect the specific views and preferences of different parts of America. If uniformity were necessary, what would be the point of having states at all?

Activist judges, disdainful of states' rights, look inside themselves, as Judge Bork warned, and fabricate new rights without any basis in the Constitution. If that document is supposed to "live and breathe," as revisionists insist, it can be reshaped to accommodate the to-do list of any faction that gets control of five seats on the Supreme Court. The problem with things that "live and breathe" is that they eventually die.

A Constitution respected by each passing generation, keeping to its unchanging principles even as societal winds change, is the best guarantor of stability and respect for law.

America is not uniquely virtuous.

In a time when the assertion of America's greatness provokes howls of outrage, it is not easy to introduce, or should we say *reintroduce*, the notion that our nation is the zenith of human achievement.

"American exceptionalism" has become a buzzword of late, embraced by those who appreciate this country's extraordinary, unsurpassed tradition of self-governance, individual rights, and earned prosperity. But the term has also drawn opposition from those who think America is overhyped.

What breeds this ambivalence, which often tips into outright hostility to our nation's history and influence? Is it some odd new strain of self-loathing, a misplaced aggression born of a deeper neurosis? Far simpler. Embracing America's past and present, especially as a strategy for a brighter future, involves something roughly half of America does not want to do—tip the hat to a set of ideas and institutions that are kryptonite to today's progressives:

- The previously mentioned Founders, who plotted a course for strong but limited government
- The faith they placed in God to guide their steps
- The virtues that made America a moral superpower, revealing the inferiority of power structures on display in other nations: communism, socialism, dictatorship, oligarchy, and more recently, Islamic extremism
- The military might that has made the world safer and freer for billions of people, not imposing an American system but clearing the land of despotic evils so that self-rule and human rights might take root

- The free markets that allow both success and failure
- The devotion to civic ritual that reinforces common values and a common language
- The confidence that our nation is a worthy model for emulation

These principles attract ridicule from certain factions defined by politics and age. Liberals, of course, have no use for them, but there is a sad generational component at work as well. Anyone young enough to have been churned through our modern education system, from kindergarten through college, has likely been scrubbed clean of the national pride that American youth once shared.

Among the kids and young adults of today, even those who are fairly fond of their nation are shy about expressing fervent admiration. It is widely perceived as obnoxious jingoism to give credit to America for what it has done for its citizens and for the world. And that's before anyone dares to suggest that this has all been ordained by God.

Giving America its due does not mean overlooking its faults. Our greatest national hymn, after all, prays "God mend thine every flaw." But the flaws are more often in our human leaders than in our constitutional edifice.

Is it the fault of the American system that we have not always fought wars, solved problems, or expanded our territory faultlessly? America's retreat from its indispensable role as a beacon for others is not the fault of the nation itself but of the leaders who have engineered this retreat and the voters who put them in power.

Even America's gravest national sins—slavery and the treatment of Indians—were committed at a time when the only thing more common than slavery around the world was tribal violence. This is not to abjure any retroactive regret for matters we might have resolved more honorably. But I recall a high school classmate's asking me, as the disease of relativism was just beginning to affect our curricula, why we were never taught to recoil at the Apaches' obliteration of a Pueblo community but were prodded into guilt over the westward progress of American civilization.

This country profited from generations of slave labor, but it also endured a horrible civil war to end it—a war that Lincoln described as a national act of atonement. And today racism is afforded no quarter in our public life.

We are a great nation not because we have committed no sins but because we have learned from them, growing into a society unequaled in achievements of value to our fellow nations. Having won liberty for ourselves and others, we face a choice of whether to continue to lead the world. How unfortunate that this is currently a topic for debate.

2

GOVERNMENT

The Constitution requires a secular society.

The Freedom from Religion Foundation is a busy shop these days, searching coast to coast for the slightest government acknowledgment that we are a nation brimming with religious history and traditions. When they discover such an affront, they descend like Furies on the offender, invoking what they see as the First Amendment's Wall of Separation between the public square and all things religious.

Except that the First Amendment erects no such wall. Congress is indeed prevented from enacting an "establishment of religion," and it has never done so. But at every level of government—local, state, and national—there is evidence of the religious faith of the American people, to the endless consternation of those who would purge religion from our history and our public life.

In America's early years, public affairs were filled with references to faith, divine providence, and the guiding hand of God. The founding generation was not reticent about the necessity of religion for a self-governing people. Familiar with the national churches "by law established" in Britain and the other kingdoms of Europe, they intended that there be no established "Church of the United States," but they left in place the various state establishments, some of which continued for several decades after the ratification of the federal Constitution. The campaign to cleanse the public square of every trace of faith reflects the prejudices of its partisans, not fidelity to the Constitution and the principles of the American founding.

Half a century ago, Madalyn Murray O'Hair, a bitter soul filled with contempt for God and his followers, led the charge against compulsory prayer in public schools. While her motives were malicious, the cause had merit. Schools' telling pupils when and how to pray is, it seems to me, an infringement of the right of parents to determine such matters for their children. The complaint that "God was kicked out of school" has always struck me as an insult to God. If juvenile misbehavior was on the rise in the 1960s, there was a long list of reasons as our culture began to rot at the edges. Telling schools to leave prayer to parents (or to kids on their own time) was probably not one of them.

But in the decades since, radical secularism has gained various footholds, purging city parks and town halls of nativity scenes and otherwise insuring that an alien who walked our streets or entered our public buildings would have no idea that the people of the United States harbored any religious beliefs whatever.

Occasionally, however, someone pushes back. In September 2015, the Freedom from Religion Foundation sent a letter to the city of Childress, Texas, demanding that the motto "In God We Trust" be removed from its police vehicles. Chief Adrian Garcia replied, "After carefully reading your letter I must deny your request for the removal of our Nation's motto from our patrol units, and ask that you and the Freedom from Religion Foundation go fly a kite."[1]

Other resistance to the FFRF and its fellow secularists has been more conventional, taking the form of legal challenges that have often found that governments are in fact permitted to reflect the religious values and practices of states and communities.

Congress begins its day with prayer, while across the street the Supreme Court decides cases in a building bearing the image of Moses. This does not amount to government imposition of religious doctrine. The display of the Ten Commandments or a Christmas crèche inhibits no citizen who would proudly assert his atheism or agnosticism. These images simply say, "This community celebrates Christmas" or "This nation was founded by people who held this faith." No one of a different view is consigned to a lower class of citizenship.

Our Constitution requires a secular government, but not a godless people.

Government is the best safety net for the needy.

What did we do before government got into what the economist Walter Williams calls the "benevolence industry"?

Do we want government to impose just enough law to keep chaos at bay, otherwise leaving us alone to enjoy our liberties to the fullest? Or do we desire a taxpayer-funded superstore of handouts that sucks the self-reliance and work ethic out of its dependents, depriving them of the best tools for escaping poverty?

Franklin D. Roosevelt offered the country an expansionist, collectivist government that would fill the bellies of all who sucked at its teat. The hardships of the Great Depression led Americans to believe that the efforts of churches and private charities were inadequate to the challenge of such widespread want. By the 1940s, federal spending had exploded—ignited by the war effort, a moral necessity, and by an epic contradiction in terms: government charity.

Dr. Williams is fond of pointing out that the federal government is constitutionally bound to spend what it takes from its citizens only on specifically enumerated objects, which do not include altruism. He properly defines charity as individuals' choosing to give of themselves to help others, not the obligation to funnel your income to Washington for disbursement by elected officials.

We have been numbed by nearly a century of looting for social programs that are rotten with waste and fraud. It is probably too glib to suggest that any job handed over to government will be poorly performed, but this one surely has been.

A generation after Roosevelt, Lyndon Johnson gave us the "Great Society" and the "War on Poverty," names that would bulge with comic irony if the results were not in fact so depressing. Twenty-two trillion dollars later, we see a nation far less self-sufficient than in 1964, when LBJ declared "unconditional war on poverty in America,"[2] and no less poor. As Ann Coulter has remarked, "Where's the exit strategy out of *that* quagmire?"

Small government is cruel.

Any attempt to reduce the explosive growth of government will be met with scolding accusations of heartlessness. The premise that only government can care for the truly needy has a corollary: that reducing the size and scope of government will lead to mass suffering.

Hysterical resistance to reform is not limited to entitlement spending. Reduce education spending and our children, we're warned, will be untaught. End federal subsidies and the economy will collapse. Take health care out of government hands and people will die. Limit environmental regulations to what's reasonable and the whole planet will die.

Civil discourse is difficult with opponents who suggest that only their ideas can fend off vast ruin. But here's an apocalyptic scenario that actually is playing out before our eyes: the American economy is headed for extinction unless we get control of spending.

One can understand the appeals of Roosevelt's spending in the midst of a brutal depression and a war for national survival. It was less excusable to stay that perilous course a generation later, as leaders told us poverty could be defeated with enormous outlays of taxpayer dollars.

But fifty years after that, uncontrolled spending by both parties threatens us with a fiscal calamity on a par with Greece's, and we still can't absorb the message that government is too big and spends too much? That's a massive perceptual disorder brought on by the decay of our national character. Add the addictive effect of free stuff paid for with other people's money, and our culture of dependency is complete. Is it too late to turn back? It is hard to be the politician who tells people, "We want the government to do less for you." Even if it is accompanied by the promise of keeping more of our money and our liberties, we pass on that offer every time, preferring government funding for countless things that are best performed by the private sector. How many Americans would accept a retroactive offer to give up Social Security benefits in return for keeping every dime they paid in and investing it themselves? The smart ones would.

Government should help us.

Ronald Reagan joked that the most frightening words in the English language are "I'm from the government, and I'm here to help you."

We laugh lest we cry. Government "help" has brought us economic ruin, deprived us of our basic rights, and needlessly stoked racial animosity. If government really wants to help, it should take care of a short list of constitutionally enumerated responsibilities and then get out of our way.

We've addressed the courts' pernicious habit of social engineering. Let's consider how our presidents and Congress have collaborated in the same pursuit. Free markets have been turned on their ears because too many politicians—and, apparently, voters—can't stand the thought of free citizens producing and consuming as they think best. Where's the fun in that for environmental alarmists who want to subsidize otherwise unviable "green" energy technologies? Where's the benefit to educrats who want all the money and all the power they can grab in their quest to teach our children without pesky competition? And free markets are the purest argument against government-run health care.

President Obama says the message of the free market is "You're on your own." In a strong and mature nation, we *are* on our own, free to enjoy individual rights and achievements. There is a small list of protections we are supposed to rely on government for, but an American life was envisioned from the start as an adventure fueled by the strengths and talents of the individual. Does that mean people should pursue their—*gasp*—"self-interest"? Yes, actually, and that is not a bad thing. In that pursuit, relying on brains and virtue, we help ourselves and others.

The produce aisle is full of vegetables not because farmers wanted to do something nice for the grocer. The growers wanted to sell them; the store wanted to buy them. Our purchase of those vegetables from the store is not an act of mutual beneficence. We want to eat, and the store wants a profit. No one is acting purely to make anyone else happy, and that's how everyone can actually wind up happy. All parties in this example are pleased to have engaged in mutually beneficial behavior, but it is market instincts, not magnanimity, that make it work.

Nothing screws up our lives like government deciding what is best for us. Wise leaders leave those decisions to us, respecting our choices within the law. It is none of government's business what mileage a car gets, what kind of light bulbs we choose, or whether a bank or car company succeeds or fails. The habits that lead to success and failure are equally instructive, producing smarter businesses and consumers.

But our government doesn't leave those choices to us. It wants to take care of us for life, as it occasionally admits. Barack Obama's reelection campaign of 2012 produced an online storybook called *The Life of Julia*—a hymn to the nanny state that was an unintentional exercise in self-parody. There's nothing blameworthy or even unconventional in Julia's life (although the milestones depicted include bearing a child but not getting married), but the moral of the story is that without the government's ever-present helping hand she would be damaged, destitute, or dead. As my friend and radio colleague Bill Bennett observed, "Notably absent in her story is any relationship with a husband, family, church, or community.... Instead, the state has taken their place and is her primary relationship."[3]

Far from a threat to the citizen, the limited government that our nation's Founders designed is the most reliable resource for the liberty and prosperity of all.

3

ENERGY

We are running out of oil.

Jimmy Carter was wrong about a lot of things, but never more spectacularly than when, at the beginning of his malaise-inducing presidency, he warned, "The oil and natural gas we rely on for 75 percent of our energy are running out.... Early in the 1980s the world will be demanding more oil than it can produce.... We could use up all the oil in the world by the end of the next decade."[1] But let history cut him some slack on this one. In 1977 almost no one suspected that an energy revolution just over the horizon would have the world swimming in oil by the early twenty-first century.

We pay so much attention to the Middle East that it's easy to forget that incalculable reserves of oil lie underneath Russia, the Americas, Africa, and the Arctic. A 2012 study by researchers at

Harvard—hardly a hotbed of fossil-fuel advocacy—exhaustively examined actual and potential exploration fields all over the world, predicting a 20 percent increase in global oil production by 2020.[2]

We have learned how to find oil and gas reserves we could never see before, and we have learned how to extract them in ways that were previously unimaginable, making the prospect of energy exhaustion just a bad dream. The planet's store of fossil fuels will last into the foreseeable future and perhaps beyond.

Bountiful reserves don't justify a cavalier attitude about the environment, of course. Proper stewardship of the earth demands that we explore and develop renewable energy sources that actually work. But in the meantime, we can't ignore the reality that fossil fuels are still the foundation of our civilized life.

Shale oil, tar sands, and hydraulic fracturing of oil and gas deposits are new frontiers that can yield prodigious benefits for the entire world. Particularly in America, where we have an understandable concern about securing energy from nations rife with jihadists, new technologies give us a real shot at energy independence and the accompanying economic and national security benefits.

Spreading gloom about our energy prospects forty years ago was one thing. Doing so today is nothing less than fraud.

Fossil fuels are bad.

Do you remember which president first told us in a State of the Union address that our nation was "addicted to oil"? It wasn't the dour Jimmy Carter or the good-timin' Bill Clinton. It wasn't even the preachy Barack Obama, though it's certainly one of his favorite themes.

The year was 2006, and the president was the career oil man George W. Bush. Bowing to the green fashions of the day, he chose a word—"addicted"—that demonized fossil fuels. He could have said quite truthfully that America *relies* on oil, but "addicted" suggests an unhealthy, even dangerous, preoccupation. The whole world relies on the fuels that God himself placed under our feet in such abundance. Our proper use of those fuels deserves a better characterization.

There were hybrid cars in 2006, but mass-produced electric cars were still four years away. Even though gas prices and other market forces would induce plenty of Americans to shell out for those high-priced technologies, President Bush declared such choices a moral imperative: "We must also change how we power our automobiles," he scolded.[3]

One could ask, then or now: Why, exactly? A presidential suggestion to welcome more energy-efficient vehicles is fine. A dire warning that we *must* change how we power our cars is an offense to liberty and logic.

The push to prematurely wean mankind from fossil fuels is not simply unwise. It's a death wish. Renouncing the fuel that sustains modern life would sentence vast populations to poverty and starvation. A later chapter on climate misconceptions will reveal the dark motivations of those who seek to do just that. Even a cursory review of recent progress clears the oil and gas industries of the charges that extremists level against them. The technology that has shown us how to explore for more American energy has also shown us how to use it more cleanly. Some alternative fuels show promise, but none yet approaches the reliability necessary to take the place of fossil fuels.

Of course we care about the planet. But those banging the drum for de-fossilization in the near term deserve to be questioned about how much they care for the people who inhabit it.

Fracking should be banned.

One of the great revolutions in the history of energy is the emergence of hydraulic fracturing—"fracking," for short. The oil boom of the early twentieth century involved drilling straight down until liquid oil gushed out. The current oil and gas boom involves technology unimagined at that time: drilling into subterranean rock (making ninety-degree turns along the way!) and injecting liquid at enormous pressure into its fissures, forcing out the oil or gas deposited there.

The fracking revolution has benefited every American, whether directly through a mineral-rights royalty check or indirectly through lower energy costs. And those benefits are precisely what have motivated anti-fracking zealots, armed with dubious claims of fracking's dangers.

This is not to say that fracking is risk-free. The water shot into the earth is mixed with chemicals to improve its fracturing efficiency. Safely processing and removing wastewater is the responsibility of the frackers. And they have risen to the challenge, encouraged by laws requiring disclosure of the chemicals used and greater oversight of the wells where it occurs.

From old-school oil wells to modern fracking rigs, the extraction of energy always affects the environment. The question is whether fracking poses dangers that outweigh its substantial benefits. The answer is a resounding *no*—and experience and technology are only going to improve that balance.

We should subsidize alternative energy.

Politicians seem to know only one way to show support for something: throw money at it. Grants, subsidies, rules, regulations, and other government schemes indicate what our leaders want us to do. It is a fact of life for all of us taxpayers that sometimes our dollars go to things we don't like.

But on matters that should be decided by individuals, government does best to butt out. Elected officials may cajole us toward their preferred environmental choices, but the responsibility is ours to vote with our dollars for the ways we wish to fuel our cars, heat our homes, and run our lives.

Government intrusion into that process produces debacles like Solyndra, the fraud-ridden California solar technology firm that collapsed in 2011, taking hundreds of millions of taxpayer dollars with it. Politicians can't resist picking winners and losers by ladling out subsidies and guaranteed loans. The problem is their uncanny proclivity to pick the losers. There are plenty of companies cranking out solar panels for people who want to pay for them. There is no need for Washington to stick its nose into that relationship.

No grant or subsidy was needed to get Americans rushing to Toyota dealerships to buy Prius hybrids. Four-dollar gas did the trick. Individuals are living more environmentally friendly lives, businesses know the benefits of greener operations, and pollution is dwindling by the generation.

But for the sworn enemies of fossil fuels, it's not enough. These busybodies are relentless in their efforts to tilt the marketplace toward unproved and unpopular technologies. It is far wiser to develop technologies that actually work. Electric cars, solar-paneled roofs, and buses running on natural gas are no longer the stuff of tree-hugger fantasies. Those technologies work for some people, and they are flocking to them.

As our energy future unfolds, many may continue to want cars that run on gas and homes heated by oil. Those choices deserve respect as well. If gas-powered cars go the way of the horse-drawn carriage on our streets, let it be because consumers made the choice, not because of the green tyranny of elected officials.

4

IMMIGRATION

The U.S. economy depends on illegal immigration.

"America is a nation of immigrants."

"Our nation was built with immigrant labor."

"Immigration has made our nation great."

All worthy points. And all invoked these days in defense of *illegal* immigration, a threat to our economy, our security, and our national identity.

Suggestions that America should enjoy secure borders and enforce its immigration laws are attacked as racist and xenophobic—and that's just for starters. Opponents of secure borders often double down, identifying illegal aliens as a vital resource, without which the American economy would collapse.

Liberals know that illegal immigration is a steady conveyor belt of fresh Democratic voters. But the soft-borders crowd has plenty of allies in the Republican business community as well, where it is well understood that illegal immigration suppresses wages across the board, padding profits.

I can understand what drives the soft-borders Democrats. They're not concerned about protecting a distinctively American culture, which they see as parochial at best and toxic at worst, and millions of new clients for the welfare state are a bonanza for their side. But what can you say about Republicans who eagerly sacrifice their conservative principles on the altar of cheap labor?

Today's immigration debates take place in a fog of misconceptions. First, Americans will indeed do the jobs illegals currently do, but not at wages artificially depressed by our failure to control our borders. Second, illegals do indeed supply countless man-hours of labor, benefiting millions of Americans. But we somehow filled those jobs with citizens and legal residents before the floodgates opened, and we could do it again. And third, the economic benefits of an illegal underground workforce are swallowed whole by the cost of supporting a massive underclass that may be ready to work but is attracted by the food, health care, shelter, and other benefits that the American welfare state dangles in front of the world.

Taking these facts into account is not "anti-immigrant" or racist. It is the natural extension of immigration policies that actually put Americans' interests first. The moral imperative to love your neighbor does not mean inviting the whole town to live with you.

We need comprehensive immigration reform.

True immigration reform entails three steps, taken in the following order:

1. Establish resources—a wall, more border patrol, drones, whatever it takes to prevent waves of new illegal immigration.
2. Verify that the flood has indeed been stopped.
3. Then—and *only* then—begin the discussion of what to do about the millions who entered illegally, some of whom deserve deportation, others a shot at legal status.

In politics, "comprehensive" can be defined as "a type of reform offered by people who will bury you with the sheer volume of their plan so as to conceal its intent." *Comprehensive* immigration reform, accordingly, involves taking the three steps of immigration reform in reverse order.

Any measures to bring illegal immigrants "out of the shadows" before the border is secure will simply attract more of them, lured by the scent of mass forgiveness. While we wrestle with the question of "amnesty," it would be wise to find illegals who have been here a long time, crime-free and well assimilated, especially those with children, and plot a course for them to stay and work legally. This is not a promise of citizenship—that is a far higher bar we can set after we have dealt with the immediate crisis. Others will be candidates for deportation, criminals and recent arrivals at the top of that list.

These reforms must be taken in a purposeful, gradual manner. The only immediate necessity is shoring up our border, creating a more stable environment in which to make long-term plans. "Comprehensive reform" is code language for no reform at all, spoken by people who have no interest in stopping illegal immigration. If the steps above are followed responsibly, the results will indeed be comprehensive—and effective.

Birthright citizenship is in the Constitution.

This could be the shortest section in this book, consisting of one sentence: *No, it's not.* Because it's just not, any more than there's a right to abortion in the Constitution.

Courts were finding what they wished in the Constitution generations before *Roe v. Wade.* In the late-nineteenth-century immigration case *United States v. Wong Kim Ark,*[1] the Supreme Court ruled that a man in his twenties, born in San Francisco to Chinese citizens, was a U.S. citizen because his parents were U.S. residents and were not engaged in business for the Chinese government. This decision represented quite a leap from the language of the Fourteenth Amendment, ratified just thirty years earlier for the purpose of conferring citizenship on former slaves and reserving citizenship for those not merely born here but "subject to the jurisdiction" of the United States. During the congressional debate over the amendment, Senator Jacob Howard of Michigan said, "This will not, of course, include persons born in the United States who are *foreigners, aliens,* who belong to the families of foreign ministers accredited to the Government of the United States, but will include every other class of persons" (emphasis added).[2]

It was quite a stretch to apply that definition to Wong Kim Ark, even though he had lived his entire life in America. Nevertheless, the decision opened the door to so-called "birthright citizenship," which is conferred by the accident of being born on American soil, regardless of the circumstances.

There is not a shred of evidence that the Fourteenth Amendment was intended to bestow citizenship on babies born to mothers who had made their way to America for the express purpose of delivering a child. Yet that's what we've got, and birthright citizenship has spawned a booming "birth tourism" industry, where fees are paid to bring women to America solely to bring forth a citizen.

We have been played. In spite of the clear intent of those who drafted and ratified the Fourteenth Amendment, judges and activists have corrupted the meaning of American citizenship.

Opposition to amnesty is cruel.

You can insist that your gripe is only with *illegal* immigration, but unless you embrace open borders you'll be branded a heartless bigot. After all, you will hear, America was intended for every living soul who ever wanted to come here for any reason, and the enforcement of immigration laws "breaks up families."

Let's begin with those precious words at the base of the Statue of Liberty, which are flung in the face of anyone who suggests tapping the brakes on immigration. Emma Lazarus composed the moving sonnet "The New Colossus" in 1883, celebrating Lady Liberty as the "Mother of Exiles" whose torch "glows world-wide welcome." The poem closes:

> Give me your tired, your poor,
> Your huddled masses yearning to breathe free,
> The wretched refuse of your teeming shore.
> Send these, the homeless, tempest-tost to me,
> I lift my lamp beside the golden door!

Stirring words, evoking the idea that made America great. "E pluribus unum," the motto on the Great Seal of the United States, means "Out of many, one." And for decades, that was the spirit of the millions of immigrants who passed through that golden door and became Americans.

But immigration today is a vastly different enterprise. Of course there are foreigners who arrive from all over the world, who carry the same burning desire to assimilate as the immigrants of the past, who arrived willing to give their new nation precedence over the lands of their birth.

The immigrants who made America great came not purely to snag American jobs or even to escape the hazards of their failed and fractious homelands. They came to learn our language, to embrace our history and our way of life, to be reborn as Americans.

A growing America needed those new citizens. When the Statue of Liberty was erected in New York Harbor, the U.S. population had swelled by 30 percent in the prior ten years to fifty million. Compare that with the seventy-two million America has added just since 1990 to reach our current 320 million.[3] In its youth, America needed a steady flow of immigrants to become great. Now, unchecked immigration threatens that greatness.

It is ridiculous to base today's immigration policy on the status quo of a century and a half ago. Neither Miss Lazarus nor the American people and the lawmakers of that era envisioned welcoming waves of immigrants in violation of the law. To suggest that borders have meaning and our laws should be followed is not a betrayal of our national heritage.

No one knows for sure how many illegal aliens are among us. Estimates range from around ten million to thirty million or more. In any case, we have to figure out what to do with them. Mass deportation seems unlikely, especially in an era when returning people to where they came from is widely considered abusive. But surely we can agree on some dividing line between those who deserve a shot at getting right with American law and those who deserve to be shown the door.

What about the stigma of "breaking up families"? Well, no family is broken up if it goes out as united as it was when it came in. The obvious leverage sought by this emotional blackmail is to curtail deportations of adults if their children were brought in through no fault of their own. Heart-rending examples abound of teenagers nailing down straight A's, volunteering around town, and winning the admiration of their communities. Sending those parents packing is not likely to win broad support. If those parents meet the requirements for forgiveness, they will get a chance to live here legally. But in the unfortunate instances where the adults are fully deserving of deportation, the concern about family disruption is less compelling. Law-breaking often results in parents' and kids' parting ways. If Dad robs a bank or Mom runs a meth lab in the garage, no one argues that the punishment should be mitigated to maintain family unity. Parents should think about family unity before committing a crime.

The crime of entering our country unlawfully is no different. The blame for endangering the family is borne completely by parents who make their kids unwitting accessories to their crime. Until we achieve clarity on birthright citizenship, there will be kids who are actual citizens faced with the deportation of their non-citizen parents. In those cases, the parents are welcome to maintain family unity by introducing their children to the land of their fathers. It's a sad fact of life that criminals bring suffering on their innocent loved ones.

Hispanics will support only candidates with soft immigration policies.

It is an enduring mystery why so many law-abiding Hispanic Americans devalue their own honorable path to citizenship by advocating law-breaking by others. Turning a blind eye to criminal acts is inconsistent with the familiar Hispanic virtues of responsibility and community. Is there a political desire to increase the Hispanic slice of the U.S. ethnic pie, even if laws are flouted? That's pretty depressing. I prefer to revisit the countless conversations I've enjoyed with

Latino citizens who have no tolerance for the violation of immigration laws, no matter the race of the offender.

There's a sizeable middle ground of Hispanic voters who neither scoff at illegal entry nor take a hard line. They are not hostile to stronger borders, but they hesitate to vote for Republicans who will strengthen those borders because they think those Republicans are motivated by prejudice. Conservatives can speak and act without a shred of racism and still get stained with that accusation, leveled most often by liberals who would rather call opponents names than debate immigration policy with them. Many Hispanics who are socially and even economically conservative therefore vote reliably Democrat.

Fortunately, that situation is changing in some places. In Texas, Greg Abbott took 44 percent of the Hispanic vote for governor in 2014 (compared with Rick Perry's 38 percent in 2010), and U.S. Senator John Cornyn pulled more of the Hispanic vote than his Democratic opponent.

Republican candidates must simultaneously affirm the necessity of restoring respect for our borders and assure skeptics that this is not bigotry. They must explain that tolerance of all who obey our laws, irrespective of race, and intolerance of those who disobey them will make a better country for Americans of all races.

America should welcome everyone who wants to live here.

Those words at the Statue of Liberty are inspiring, speaking of a country wide open to all—or, as many conveniently forget today, all who are willing to observe our laws. But that is *so* 1883.

Immigration has become such a tangled web that even *legal* immigration requires some scrutiny. Intimidated by accusations of bigotry, many immigration reformers assure critics that they are more than eager to maintain a heavy flow of legal arrivals—"high walls but wide doors," as they say.

But is that a good idea?

One of our main economic challenges is to create jobs for the citizens we already have. In 1990, the federal government established H-1B visas for immigrants with highly specialized skills, a policy that seemed logical at the time. Maybe we *didn't* have enough skilled workers to serve the booming tech industry. Allowing companies to bring in up to sixty-five thousand foreign workers to meet that demand raised few eyebrows.

But even as American workers began to notice the downside of this policy, Congress kept pushing to widen the door. When the Immigration Innovation Bill of 2013 sought to raise the ceiling on skilled immigrants to three hundred thousand, Senator Marco Rubio scoffed at those who worried the country would be "overrun by Ph.D.s."[4]

One might expect such inclusive instincts to win bipartisan praise. But an article by Josh Harkinson that year in the usually pro-open-borders *Mother Jones* magazine stood out. "How H-1B Visas Are Screwing Tech Workers" detailed the pain of employees at the pharmaceutical giant Pfizer, which laid off hundreds with one final instruction: train your replacements freshly arrived from India.

The wife of one unemployed worker asked President Obama directly during a web chat on the subject: "My husband has an engineering degree with over ten years of experience. Why does the government continue to issue and extend H-1B visas when there are tons of Americans just like my husband with no job?"

In the summer of 2015, the same fate befell 250 employees at the Walt Disney Company in Orlando, many with long years of service, who were shown the door with the same humiliating directive: train the people we just hired so we can fire you.[5]

It is not unreasonable to ask whether even legal immigration should be seriously dialed back. We are no longer the adolescent nation that once needed a large influx of people to settle the continent and supply the workforce for an explosively growing economy. Today's economy should grow at a rate to accommodate new generations of our existing citizenry, plus any new arrivals we choose to welcome.

But how many should that be? Once we secure our borders, we might want to call a time-out on legal immigration, if only for a few years, to see if our own workers do in fact find and fill the jobs that immigrants have been taking and to relieve some of the pressure on our social safety net. A study published by the Center for Immigration Studies in 2015 found that roughly half of *legal* immigrant households receive benefits from one or more welfare programs, a higher rate of dependence than that of native households.[6]

It is a point of national pride that people from around the world seek to live here, as well as the strongest argument against those who would defame America. But even though this is "a nation of immigrants," leaving the welcome mat out for all of the world's huddled masses is proving a serious strain in the dramatically different circumstances of the twenty-first century. America may be, as Lincoln said, the "last, best hope of man on earth," but there's no reason we should have a monopoly on prosperity. We should focus on helping other nations succeed so that their peoples can enjoy the blessings of liberty at home.

5

EDUCATION

Our schools don't have enough money.

It is the nature of government to constantly reach into our pockets for more money. Bureaucracies greedily feed at the endlessly replenished trough of taxpayer dollars.

Schools are no different. We have warmer feelings for our child's second-grade teacher than we do for the clerk who rejected our paperwork at the Department of Motor Vehicles, but make no mistake—public schools are government schools with a voracious appetite for our money.

Are there school systems that need more funds? Of course there are. From inner cities to exploding suburbs, we can find schools that need fixing and expanding, and new schools that need to be built. But many of those valid needs could be met if school systems operated under the kind of austerity we should demand from all corners of government.

The big misconception is that we do not spend enough, in the aggregate, on education. If schools are suffering, it's not because we're not pouring enough money into them. Perhaps, public education being a government enterprise, the money is distributed unevenly and ineptly. But schools as a national line item are not underfunded.

Consider the public school budgets of New York, New Jersey, and Connecticut, which spend between $16,000 and $20,000 per year on each pupil. Are the schools in Arizona, Utah, and Idaho, which spend between $6,500 and $7,000 per pupil, only one-third as good? Those three states, with the smallest education budgets in the country, somehow crank out quality kids at a fraction of the cost. Sure, the cost of living is higher in New York than in Utah, but that does not account for the often inverse relationship between per-pupil spending and education quality.

W. Norton Grubb, a professor at the University of California at Berkeley, of all places, exposed the folly of equating higher spending with better education in his 2009 book *The Money Myth*. For years, he and others have been trying to tell us that the formula for good education is complex. Money is certainly part of the mix, but results depend more on the quality of a school's surrounding community, students' family lives, and factors that have nothing to do with funding—management techniques, receptivity to reform, and teacher quality.

Teachers are underpaid.

Speaking of the heroic men and women who toil year in and year out to teach our kids, no discussion of education improvements can avoid the minefield of teacher salaries.

We've all heard (or perhaps uttered) the standard lament about the difference between teachers' salaries and what professional athletes and movie stars rake in. "Is Tom Brady worth a hundred times more than Mrs. Schneider? I mean, he plays a game for a living, and she is teaching Billy how to read." No doubt about it, time spent learning from a good teacher is more valuable than time spent watching a football game or the latest *Avengers* flick. But our mistake is presuming that such a calculation is the basis for anyone's compensation.

Athletes, actors, and rock stars make what they do because they put that money right back in the hands of those who pay them, usually with a handsome profit. Mrs. Schneider may be a joy in your child's classroom, but millions of people aren't paying to watch her. The marketplace determines what each teacher, point guard, rapper, author, bricklayer, brain surgeon, and burger-flipper makes. The size of the available talent pool is another factor. There are a lot of people who can skillfully educate our kids, and God bless every one of them. The list of people who can run ExxonMobil or win a Super Bowl is not as large.

Market forces explain salaries in every job of every type at every level. An employer offers a salary of x for a particular job. If that job is filled, the system has worked, as both employee and employer are satisfied with the arrangement. In a complex system of multiple jobs at multiple levels, employers offer various salaries based on what they calculate various jobs are worth. If every job is filled, their calculations were correct, and again everyone is satisfied. If an employer offers a salary of x and the job is not filled, a higher salary is in order. This is in fact the *only* indicator that x is too low for that job. Pay is not determined by how warmly we view the profession, how demanding the work is, or how it compares with Hollywood or the NFL.

So the only question is, do we have a teacher shortage? Your local schools might. Mine may not. Nationally, the answer is almost certainly no. The National Center for Education Statistics keeps track of the college degrees awarded annually in each field. In 2013, elementary education was the eleventh-most-popular degree, with 52,030 awarded. Education ranked twenty-fifth, with 33,543; early childhood education ranked twenty-ninth, with 27,710; special education ranked thirty-sixth, with 22,692; secondary education ranked sixty-second, with 12,930; and physical education ranked sixty-fifth, with 11,689. Add 28,153 degrees in educational leadership and administration, a career likely to involve some classroom teaching along the way, and you get nearly two hundred thousand fresh graduates pouring into the teaching profession each year.

To fill how many jobs? According to the NCES's 2013 figures,[1] about ninety-three thousand, or roughly one job for every two graduates. Even allowing for some regional variation, it is a myth that we are running low on teaching talent.

So what do teachers make? For the school year ending in 2013, the national-average salary of our public elementary and secondary school teachers was $56,383. And remember, that's the *average* for teachers of every age, level of experience, and school district. That average is more than sixty-five thousand dollars in Alaska, California, Connecticut, Maryland, and New Jersey, and more than seventy thousand dollars in Massachusetts, New York, and the District of Columbia.[2]

That may strike some as ample, others as insufficient. But remember that it is for a daily grind that fills but three-fourths of the year.

(A moment to quell the revolt that always arises when someone says teachers don't work all summer. First, yes, they do, in ways any teacher will gladly describe if you ask. They will also describe the extras asked of them in the modern teaching world, which is another reason for our gratitude and admiration. I would suggest, however, that the list of workers in today's market who are asked to toil well beyond the hours for which they're officially paid is very long.)

So yes, it takes scores of American teachers' salaries to equal one paycheck of even a mid-level professional athlete, Fortune 500 CEO, or pop star. But every teacher working today chose the profession and accepted his or her job at the salary offered. The marketplace has spoken.

School choice will kill public education.

It was inevitable. As public schools began to display some of the worst characteristics of government institutions—lagging quality, unresponsiveness, resistance to reform—the customers began to revolt.

It is important to remember that our nation's Founders never envisioned the massive network of government schools that today handles fifty million kids a year. Those schools developed as our nation grew, and now that we've got them, we are entitled to hold them as accountable as other taxpayer-financed functions. We pay the bills, we run the show.

Ideally, government-run schools should meet the needs of kids and parents. But despite the laudable history of public education in America, nowadays the system frequently falls disastrously short of that ideal. During the twentieth century, a number of developments began to undermine public schools' ability to usher students efficiently and effectively from kindergarten to the threshold of college. Teachers' unions made it almost impossible to fire the incompetent. Curricula were watered down and purged of anything that would instill national pride. Discipline eroded, leaving hooligans in charge.

Against this backdrop, it's not surprising that some parents developed an appetite for alternatives. Families that could afford private schools followed that path, and the number of homeschooling families doubled from 1999 to 2013.[3] But the obligation to pay school taxes regardless of where your children are educated sparked the school choice movement, a multi-faceted revolution intended to give taxpayers more bang for the education buck.

The simplest form of school choice is the voucher system, which gives money back to families to spend as they see fit, including on eligible private schools. Teachers' unions and other guardians of the government school monopoly *hate* vouchers, warning that they will drain public schools of their captive clients and starve them into extinction. They ignore the one thing that would keep any family in a public school: excellence. Competition is life's greatest motivator. American cars improved after Detroit got its butt handed to it by foreign makers of better and cheaper cars. Fast-food restaurant menus sprouted healthier options when competitors siphoned away customers. Why would schools not react similarly?

It's the advocates of school choice who have faith in the resiliency and adaptability of public schools, while defenders of the status quo cower in fear. It's enough to make you suspect that school-choice opponents are not as interested in better schools as they are in protecting union jobs and their institutional power.

Another form of school choice, growing in popularity, is charter schools, public schools freed from the direct supervision of the local system, allowing experimentation that has inspired supporters and swayed critics. In his final year in office, President Bill Clinton pointed with pride to the expansion of charter schools during his two terms, promising additional funding for education that explored new ways to improve learning.[4]

The message is clear. Public schools, which are more accurately called *government* schools, vary in their performance as much as every other arm of government does—sometimes the taxpayer is served well, often not. But while there is no competing office to handle your car registration, families have a world of options for their kids' educations. And since we all pay taxes for schools we may or may not use, there is a strong argument for giving us options beyond the one building down the road where the school board tells us we have to send our kids.

If parents' freedom to educate their children is respected, public schools will be under greater pressure to perform. Some will fail, and some of those will close—as proper a cleansing of the marketplace as the extinction of an unsuccessful restaurant, auto maker, or bank. Even if the occasional government school lands in the ditch, demand will stimulate the creation of a better one, which will likely spring from the hard lessons learned by the prior failure. Our institutions of learning should themselves learn from good decisions and bad, just as we all do. Government is usually insulated from this process—why improve customer service if you have no competition and unlimited funds? If schools of all types can be improved by injecting more choice into the education marketplace, it is an offense against our children to deny them that choice.

Every kid needs to go to college.

I think the questions began in junior high school. "So, where will you go to college?"

I was about thirteen and more concerned about where I was going for summer vacation. But it was becoming clear that the expected framework of life included college, unless you didn't mind living under a bridge.

Looking back on those days of the early seventies, I remember that our high school had something called "the vocational wing," generally filled with the teenage toughs who smoked cigarettes (in the smoking area the school actually provided) and snagged middling grades at best. While my friends and I tested the Pythagorean theorem and hyper-analyzed Chekhov plays, they were pulling the linkage on '66 Chevys and rewiring refrigerators. As our senior year loomed, those of us in the "college preparatory" pipeline were toiling for the best grade point averages we could muster, desperate to avoid the stigma of being Kids Who Could Not Get In.

So what became of the more academically inclined? We went to college, which worked out well for most, I'm sure. I've turned my journalism degree from the University of Maryland into something I hope has been of value, and many of my friends pursued useful degrees in business, engineering, and law. There are even some who managed to blaze a functional trail with majors in philosophy or literature. But I know a lot of folks whose degrees led precisely nowhere or who followed a path quite unrelated to their college studies. In other words, among the high school graduates who went to college, some did well and at least as many wasted a lot of time and a lot of money.

Meanwhile, the kids in the vocational wing popped right out of high school with a useful skill that was instantly of value in the marketplace. Many were able to earn far more far faster than most of us Joe Colleges.

The value of skilled technical labor is even more evident today, while college has become an intellectual and moral minefield that not only fails with alarming frequency to prepare kids for the real world but actually schools them in dysfunction.

I don't want to denigrate all of higher education, still a worthy destination for many and a necessary one for several professions. But a growing number of high school graduates are delaying the immediate jump to college or bypassing it altogether, and with promising results. Some of them begin work, starting their climb up the ladder to prosperity. Some join the military, rediscovering the value of service to country that took such a pummeling during and after the Vietnam era. Some embark on travels that teach them more about our nation and the world than a classroom ever will. In short, the young person delaying or opting out of college is no longer presumed to be lazy.

Parents huddling with their sons and daughters over college catalogues must exercise great caution today. The institution that will confer a degree in their chosen field of study may also poison their patriotism, their economic common sense, and the values their parents have labored to instill. There are women's studies majors that are not about womanhood but hatred of men (and conservative women). There are black studies majors that are not about blackness but hatred of whites (and conservative blacks). There are majors in social work that are inimical to society and work. Many other majors are little more than funnels of leftist indoctrination.

I am blessed to be a broadcasting colleague of the former education secretary and drug czar Bill Bennett, who with our mutual friend David Wilezol wrote the enormously valuable *Is College Worth It?*, detailing not just the hazards of modern higher education but also its staggering cost. Educated in the liberal arts, both authors have made the most of their learning, but they recognize that higher education is desperately in need of reform and that a college degree is no longer an imperative.

Is this reassessment simply a reflection of conservative frustration with the liberalism that has long pervaded our universities? Robert Reich, Bill Clinton's secretary of labor, a longtime academic, and a liberal's liberal writes, "A four-year college degree isn't necessary for many of tomorrow's good jobs," calling for "a world-class system of vocational and technical education." If Reich and Bennett agree on something, it deserves serious consideration.

6

THE BUSINESS WORLD

Capitalism is bad.

This section requires that I reveal a dark secret for any conservative broadcaster: one of my earliest industry heroes was Phil Donahue.

From my teen years to young adulthood, I watched countless *Donahue* shows, which covered the widest imaginable range of topics with an unequaled panoply of guests. As I jumped into the ocean of talk radio in the early 1980s, I strove to imitate his versatility and unpredictability.

Phil enjoyed guests who disagreed with him, and that's certainly what he got in 1979 when he welcomed another hero of mine, the economist Milton Friedman. The Nobel laureate delivered a concise defense of free-market capitalism which still circulates today. Phil had set up a premise with his usual skill, confronting his guest with a litany of global ills: wealth disparities, poverty, greed, inordinate concentrations of power—the poisoned fruits of capitalism that years later would become staples of Bernie Sanders's campaign speeches.

That day, a year before Reagan's 1980 victory, Friedman carved a gem of an answer that every lover of freedom should memorize:

> The world runs on individuals pursuing their separate interests. The great achievements of civilization have not come from government bureaus. Einstein did not construct his theory under order from a bureaucrat. Henry Ford didn't revolutionize the automobile industry that way. In the only cases in which the masses have escaped from the kind of grinding poverty you're talking about, the only cases in recorded history, are where they have had capitalism and largely free trade.

As Donahue sprouted a few more grey hairs, Friedman continued: "If you want to know where the masses are worst off, it's exactly in the kinds of societies that depart from that."

Skillfully shredded before an audience of millions: the notion that people are better off when government tries to equalize incomes and act as mastermind of the economy.

"The record of history is absolutely crystal clear," Friedman continued, "that there is no alternative way so far discovered of improving the lot of ordinary people that can hold a candle to the productive activity unleashed by a free enterprise system."

Phil politely pushed back, objecting that capitalism "seems to reward not virtue as much as ability to manipulate the system." Friedman asked where reward for virtue ever shows up in an economic model: "You think the Communist commissar rewards virtue? You think a Hitler rewards virtue?" Then the eyebrow-raiser: "If you'll pardon me, do you think

American presidents reward virtue? Do they choose their appointees on the basis of the virtue of the people appointed or on the basis of their political clout? Is it really true that political self-interest is nobler somehow than economic self-interest?" He concluded with a question any critic of capitalism should be made to answer: "Just tell me where in the world you find these angels who are going to organize society for us?"

Friedman passed away in 2006, but YouTube is forever.[1]

No government has the moral foundation to pass judgment on the economic free will of citizens. America and the world are suffering from the benevolent poison of leaders who think they know what's best for us.

C. S. Lewis was not an economist, but his understanding of human nature gave him deeper insight into our economic system than many a so-called expert:

> Of all tyrannies, a tyranny sincerely exercised for the good of its victims may be the most oppressive. It would be better to live under robber barons than under omnipotent moral busybodies. The robber baron's cruelty may sometimes sleep, his cupidity may at some point be satiated; but those who torment us for our own good will torment us without end for they do so with the approval of their own conscience.[2]

Capitalism only seems "greedy" to those who think they have better ideas for your wealth and property than you do.

Big business ignores the interests of real people.

In August 2011, a year before he won the Republican nomination for president, Mitt Romney almost blew it. Facing hecklers at the

Iowa State Fair, he responded to their demand for higher corporate tax rates: "Corporations are people, my friend." He had given the Democrats a rhetorical club to beat him with, but Romney was right. As he explained to the hecklers, "Everything corporations earn ultimately goes to people. Where do you think it goes?"

Corporations are indeed made up of people, and they serve people. They employ people. They provide goods and services for people. They protect health and save lives. They build things that keep our nation safe. Some people in corporate structures earn massive salaries that, compared with the wages of entry-level workers, might seem "unfair." But corporate salaries can be set either by the job market's relentlessly impartial laws of supply and demand or by politicians and bureaucrats. Plenty of countries have tried the latter system, and their experience hasn't given "fairness" a good name.

Anti-business ravings are usually rooted in the idea that the mere existence of wealthy people is the cause of everyone else's troubles. This is a curious notion, since millions of people have gotten an entry-level job because some large corporation was there to give it to them. In most cases, they have done what you're supposed to do with an entry-level job—they entered. Then they grew, improved, and climbed the ladder. Maybe they changed ladders and climbed to success in other companies. Maybe they learned something in that climb that spurred them to start their own companies. This notion that American big business is a millstone around the neck of the working class is a crock. America's middle class would not exist without the jobs, products, and services that come from our large corporations.

The people who run these corporations, being human, sometimes misbehave. They may cheat, lie, steal, and display repulsive greed. This is why there are laws to restrain such habits.

Huge businesses can lack the personal touch found in smaller companies, producing anecdotes of workers who somehow ran afoul of "the system." But most employees who have a bad experience at Company A emerge tougher and smarter, perhaps taking those lessons across the street to Company B. That's the beauty of a free economy—there's always a better company out there to work for. The larger companies have big buildings, big budgets, and sometimes big hierarchies, but they are all the product of people. Those people are all trying to do the same thing—succeed. They want success for customers and stockholders.

Sometimes businesses must downsize to survive, which can leave a trail of news stories featuring workers resentful of the marketplace that just laid them off. This is completely understandable, but it doesn't mean the system is rigged against the working classes. The food we eat, the gas in our cars, the products throughout our homes all came from people working to make a living by helping us enjoy a standard of living no country has ever matched. Many of them work for enormous companies. Whenever we hear someone demonize corporations, we should imagine life without them.

Corporations should pay more taxes.

The politics of envy demands confiscatory tax rates for the wealthy on the grounds that "they can afford it," and the same rationale fuels attacks on businesses.

This is stunningly shortsighted. Companies have an option that individual citizens generally do not—increasing their income by raising prices. If taxes go up, businesses pass the cost on to the public, making the business tax increase an eventual burden to consumers at all income levels.

High corporate taxes are also a disincentive to doing business in America. We make a habit of wagging fingers at companies that move operations and resources to other countries, so here's an idea: How about making America's tax structure less hostile? There is a reason most of the 2016 Republican presidential field unveiled tax plans featuring a reduction of corporate tax rates. The resulting boost in jobs and productivity can actually result in *more* revenue. Higher profits mean higher tax revenues. A larger and better-paid workforce earns more taxable income. Reducing tax rates to increase tax receipts may seem counterintuitive, but it has worked four times in the past hundred years—in the 1920s, the '60s, the '80s, and the first decade of this century.

Tax cuts are associated with Republicans, but one of the best explanations of why they work comes from a Democrat—one of the last who showed any understanding of the economic facts of life. In 1962, John F. Kennedy told the Economic Club of New York:

> Our true choice is not between tax reduction, on the one hand, and the avoidance of large Federal deficits on the other. It is increasingly clear that no matter what party is in power, so long as our national security needs keep rising, an economy hampered by restrictive tax rates will never produce enough revenues to balance our budget just as it will never produce enough jobs or enough profits.... In short, it is a paradoxical truth that tax rates are too high today and tax revenues are too low and the soundest way to raise the revenues in the long run is to cut the rates now.

What JFK said a half-century ago is true today. Reducing tax burdens unleashes the kind of activity that makes an economy grow. What do businesses want to do? Make more profit. What do they do with that additional profit? Engage in more of the behavior that produced that profit. This is true of a Fortune 500 company and of the Mom-and-Pop shop down the street. It is a terrible idea to treat business income as money growing on a tree for a ravenous government to harvest. Let businesses keep more of what they earn and they will expand, generating the jobs and growth that are the only hope for reviving our gasping economy.

Walmart is evil.

The enemies of the free market and consumer choice have found a favorite whipping boy—Walmart. Founded in the early 1960s by Arkansan Sam Walton, the giant retailer is now the world's largest private employer and its top revenue producer.[3] The two simple reasons for Walmart's success—the enormous number of people who want to shop there and the enormous number who want to work there—drive some people crazy.

Sam Walton redefined retail in America, achieving stunning efficiency and passing the savings on to consumers, who come back again and again to reap those savings. Walmart's customers benefit along with the company.

Revolutions are often messy. Small stores—usually local family businesses—panic at the arrival in their neighborhood of a Walmart, which stocks far more items at much lower cost. But Walmart is as subject to the free market as anyone else. Small businesses can offer many things a behemoth like Walmart can't, like personal service, unique products, and instant response to consumer tastes. The smartest small businesses, having maximized those strengths, are thriving in the age of big-box retail.

Meanwhile, Walmart saves American shoppers billions of dollars per year while offering jobs for 1.3 million Americans, 2.2 million persons worldwide. So with those numbers in our heads, let's examine the plight of that workforce.

Labor unions despise Walmart, which may be all you need to know to admire it. Unions thrive on adversarial relations between labor and management that make workers dependent on them. Walmart's employees routinely reject opportunities to fork over big chunks of their paychecks for union dues. The unions weave conspiracy theories of managers poised to punish a recalcitrant workforce should it opt for union tutelage. The truth is that the Walmart business model allows for input and communication up the management ladder, reducing the appeal of paying an intermediary to resolve workplace disputes.

Walmart workers are at least as happy as those at any other massive retail employer, often more so. And Walmart customers are even happier, as the company's bottom line shows. My talk-show colleague Mike Gallagher offers an explanation of Walmart's appeal in the form of some rhetorical questions:

> Who would you rather have delivering your health care? The federal government? Or Walmart? Who would you rather have running the local school system? The local teachers' union? Or Walmart? Who would you rather have delivering the *mail*, for heaven's sake?[4]

Walmart's detractors are merely reacting to the instructive light the company sheds on some of their wayward beliefs.

7

HEALTH CARE

"Free" health care works—just ask the British, the Canadians, and the Cubans!

No product or service is "free." Few things, in fact, are as expensive as the free housing, free college, free health care, free you-name-it that statists want to provide for everyone. What is free for some is paid for by others, and it's funneled through the sigmoid colon of government—a guarantee that the money will be sloppily spent with little accountability.

Unlike households or businesses, which quickly detect the consequences of overspending, government enjoys the power to tax, which it can exercise at will and without restraint, egged on by voters who receive the fruits of others' labor. In the words of George Bernard

Shaw, "A government that robs Peter to pay Paul can always rely on the support of Paul."

We can debate the prudence or even the morality of the government's providing everything that people need, but there is little doubt that government runs many things badly, especially the things best left to the private sector. There is no example with higher stakes than our health care system.

Obamacare became law in the United States after a successful campaign to deceive Americans into thinking that health care would be improved by de-emphasizing market influences and handing much of the system over to government control. There were plenty of anecdotes available to grease this lie—consumers' struggles with private insurance, harrowing tales of living without coverage. Yet it was not our health care system that needed reforming; it was our insurance system.

But for Obamacare's cheerleaders, the ultimate goal is to control as much of our lives as possible. Knowing that many voters had faced daunting problems with medical bills, they proposed a Utopia of affordable insurance, no denials of coverage, and generous subsidies for all. Lest anyone suspect this was too good to be true, they talked about other lands whose happy people get all the health care they need at no cost. The promise of "free" health care should call to mind a basic truth: you get what you pay for.

Take Great Britain, whose National Health Service has long been held up as a shining model for America. It looks appealing until you examine its track record. That free visit to the doctor may not take place when you need it, if at all. The only way to pay for everybody's "free" treatment is to ration the care dispensed.

The British system, replicated in Canada, becomes a minefield for those who require further treatment after that happy no-cost first visit. That's when patient care becomes more expensive and therefore rare. Canadians pour across our borders for a level of care they cannot dream of receiving under their single-payer system.

Sally Pipes, a British scholar at the Pacific Research Institute, writing in *Forbes* in 2011, exposed the fraud of "guaranteed" access to care in Britain:

> The NHS is broken, and not in some superficial way that a simple tweak would fix. The incentives are wrong. The government's main priority is keeping costs low—not providing quality care. Patients can't choose how they receive their care—it's one-size-fits-all medicine. And the entrenched NHS bureaucracy has no reason to improve efficiency.[1]

Four years later, the Care Quality Commission, the official watchdog for the NHS, reported on the continuing erosion of care in British hospitals: two-thirds of them offer substandard care, three-quarters have safety problems, and all of them are bracing for further budget cuts—twenty-two billion pounds by 2020. "Too many patients are already receiving care that is unacceptably poor, unsafe or highly variable in its quality," reported the *Guardian*.[2]

At least the British government tries to evaluate its health care system honestly. The same can't be said for Cuba, another hyped medical paradise that has been the object of intense admiration by the Left. No one is surprised, of course, if a communist regime lies, even outrageously, about its achievements. No one, that is, except Michael Moore, whose 2007 documentary *Sicko* is an indictment of American health care and a salute to the Cuban variety. To illustrate the delights of Castro's system, he ferried a boatload of patients across the Straits of Florida to get a taste of that enviable Havana health care. "I asked them to give us the same exact care they give their fellow Cuban citizens, no more, no less—and that's what they did," he narrates. The Castro PR machine, however, played Moore like a fiddle, escorting him through a showplace hospital reserved for what passes for Cuba's upper class.

John Stossel, in a biting segment of ABC's *20/20*, exposed the famed director as the Castros' dupe, showing that the facts of Cuban heath care differ starkly from Moore's narrative.[3] Photos of more representative clinics revealed horrific conditions that no American hospital would tolerate. The regime's boast about the island's low infant mortality rate is a case of statistical sleight of hand: the numbers are artificially depressed by aborting unhealthy fetuses and not recording the births of babies who die soon after delivery. Moore's figures for Cuban life expectancy, coming from the regime itself, are likewise utterly unreliable.

Socialized health care systems are crumbling around the world. The Democrats, paying lip service to the private marketplace to get Obamacare passed, promised us it was something different. The more candid among their ranks acknowledge that single-payer care is in fact their goal. Liberals never pause to say, "Okay, we've made some progress. Before going further, let's see how this works." The increasingly obvious unworkability of the Affordable Care Act, rather than inducing a little humility, spurs the Left to finish the job of socializing the medical system that was the envy of the world. We don't have long to reverse course.

The Affordable Care Act is working beautifully.

In June 2015, with a crowd of Republicans preparing to run for president on a pledge of repealing Obamacare, the law's namesake announced that the federal takeover of the health care market was working great—even better than expected!

The accuracy of that claim depends, of course, on how you measure success. If the goal is to anesthetize a compliant nation and send it sleepwalking down the path to single-payer, the president may well have been right. Since the ink on Obama's signature dried, many Americans have lost the sense of urgency to repeal this monstrosity. A better measure of the Affordable Care Act's success would be the number of enrollees. The *Washington Examiner*'s review of the numbers from 2015 does not exactly suggest a law working "better than expected":

> When Obamacare was passed in March 2010, the Congressional Budget Office had projected that enrollment in the law's insurance exchanges would grow from 8 million in 2014, to 13 million in 2015, and then jump to 21 million by 2016 (a projection that was reiterated in its most recent report). But as of [June 2015], HHS says that just 10.2 million signed up and paid premiums (which only met HHS's downwardly revised target). That means that the number of enrollees will have to double next year to meet CBO projections of 21 million.[4]

The much-hyped rollout of ACA, even with its online disasters, presumably attracted a wave of initial signups by the curious. A doubling of the number of enrollees in the calendar year 2016 was therefore wildly unrealistic. Nevertheless, the failure to meet projections is instructive. Many are delaying or avoiding signing up because they have heard—or experienced—the messy stories about the health law's incursions into our lives, our health, and our choices.

Insurance companies, forced to cover anyone and everyone, are jacking premiums to the moon or canceling coverage altogether. Blue Cross Blue Shield of Texas, for instance, dumped 367,000 customers from its individual plans after losing four hundred million dollars. One of those customers was the wife of Merrill Matthews of the Institute for Policy Innovation. As he wrote in *Forbes*, Blue Cross suggested switching to an Obamacare-compliant plan, which they offered, but the premium would have more than doubled. The only relief available entailed stratospheric deductibles or changing to a smaller network of providers, which did not include Mrs. Matthews's doctor.[5]

Ironically enough, the young Americans who were crucial to President Obama's two electoral victories are bearing a particularly heavy burden under Obamacare. As Diana Furchtgott-Roth and Jared Meyer of the Manhattan Institute have pointed out, single millennials are forced to buy expensive coverage they do not need. The researchers profiled one young professional man, childless and of sound mind and good habits, who was railroaded into a policy containing maternity care, pediatric dental services, mental health coverage, and substance-abuse treatment.[6]

In light of sharply rising premiums, many healthy young people will quite rationally choose to forgo health insurance and pay the Obamacare fine for failure to comply with the "individual mandate." There will never be enough healthy young people in the system to cover the cost of older people, who consume far more medical care. Obamacare is a recipe for the painfully rationed care on display in Britain and Canada.

Employers obliged to cover full-time employees will simply reduce the number of full-time employees. In early 2014, I asked my radio listeners if they were seeing what I was seeing in my own industry of broadcasting—salaried workers cut back to twenty-nine hours per week, just shy of the thirty hours at which medical coverage is mandatory. In this area at least, the laws of economics are as inexorable as the laws of physics.

Health care is not a right. It is a responsibility. Health insurance is a commodity that functioning adults secure for themselves and their families. They can do so most efficiently in a free market offering competitive plans delivering the most options to patients and doctors alike.

Efforts to repeal and replace Obamacare are noble and necessary. But to win favor with a public that may be getting used to it, opponents must offer attractive alternatives. That will likely mean scouring the Affordable Care Act for the stray line item that is actually workable. The facet of the ACA that may be a part of a bipartisan successor involves rules on covering previously existing conditions. In addition, many Americans have grown fond of the depressing notion of allowing young adults to stay on their parents' policy until the age of twenty-six.

In the summer of 2013, President Obama feigned openness with an offer to consider Republican suggestions for health care reform. "If they have better ideas," he said, "I'm happy to hear them. But I haven't heard any so far." It makes you wonder if the Oval Office has a computer and an Internet connection. A ten-year-old could collect a dozen thoughtful conservative proposals with a few clicks. In fact, there may be too many proposed alternatives. Opponents of Obamacare may need to coalesce behind some easy-to-digest principles that a wide section of Americans can support.

Obamacare is the law of the land—just let it go.

"The law of the land."

The term—suggesting unquestioned permanence—is often wielded to shut down discussion of unjust laws or erroneous rulings. But Obamacare will cease to be the law of the land the moment a future president signs the legislation repealing it. Today, nearly every Republican politician is outspoken in his call to "repeal and replace," knowing that millions of Americans want just that.

The question is how many millions? Enough to win a presidential election? Any Democratic president would thwart the repeal of Obamacare, but even a Republican would confront a bewildering array of alternatives and obstacles in wresting health care out of the government's hands and giving it back to doctors, patients, and insurance companies in a free market.

Conservatives are powerfully disappointed that the Republicans who won control of Congress in 2014 failed to mount a serious challenge to Obamacare. Senator Ted Cruz's galvanizing efforts notwithstanding, the numbers were not there for the supermajority needed to override the certain presidential veto.

Health care policy is complex, and people's responses depend on their jobs, their personal circumstances, and their own health histories. Reforms that may strike one voter as sound can scare the pants off a neighbor. The dismantling of Obamacare therefore needs to be accompanied by the promise of something that will work better for most people.

But how to phrase that? A good first step is to identify the gripes most people have with the health care system and pitch reform as the best way to address those complaints. Millions of Americans are facing higher premiums; more still complain about the inability of doctors and patients to chart a course unmolested by bureaucrats. These concerns should guide reformers in offering solutions to the costs and burdens of health care, many of which have gotten worse since the passage of the ACA.

You don't have to be a conservative to recognize that market competition brings down prices. Repeal-and-replace proposals should focus on insurance reform, offering more choices to more consumers. Allowing insurers to compete across state lines is a concept Americans of many political stripes can accept, especially if they have seen their premiums increase despite Obama's empty promises of affordability.

Health savings accounts keep decision-making (and money) in the hands of taxpayers, resulting in more honest market transactions that keep prices down. One reason our hospital bills feature fifteen-dollar Tylenol tablets is that insurance companies have routinely paid for them.

Tax credits could empower citizens to purchase health care plans at more affordable market rates. Knowing that companies can shop more widely, insurers will offer better deals to businesses, which can pass the savings on to their employees.

Americans' initial shock and anger over Obamacare is dwindling, but as costs rise and choices dwindle, discontent will build, offering a new president and a new Congress an opportunity to get government as far out of the health care business as possible.

8

LIFE

Abortion is between a woman and her doctor.

Slavery persisted in the United States because of the presumption that the slave was not a full-fledged human person, one of those endowed by their Creator with the unalienable rights of life, liberty, and the pursuit of happiness. When the personhood of the slave was recognized, slavery became intolerable.

Abortion is tolerated only if society denies the distinct humanity of the unborn. "It's not really a baby," goes the pro-choice argument, even though the moment a wanted pregnancy is announced, that's exactly what the new life is called. "When will you hear the baby's heartbeat?" "No wine for me, it could harm the baby." Well, is it a baby or not?

The microscopic organism newly implanted in the wall of the uterus looks very different from the crying, wriggling infant taking its first breath after birth. But it is a discrete member of the human species, bearing its own unique genetic identity, and will grow into what everyone would call a baby if left alone.

Supporters of abortion rights may make any arguments they please, but they cannot rationally say that the issue is "between a woman and her doctor," as if she is seeking to have a mole lasered off. They may *wish* the issue to be left solely to women seeking abortions and the doctors willing to perform them, and that is what the law currently allows. But as long as there is breath in the lungs of one pro-life American, there will be a battle to allow air into the lungs of every baby who would otherwise be condemned by its mother.

Let that word sink in. *Mother.* That's what every pregnant woman is, like it or not. There is a new life in her womb, a life that depends on her for everything. Of course there are unwanted pregnancies, and the circumstances can be complex and distressing. But the question is whether the shock of the unwanted pregnancy will be compounded by the needless taking of a life.

Whenever someone asserts that abortion is "between a woman and her doctor," imagine a voiceless child, unable to plead for that first breath or the promise of the life to follow. The pro-life movement sees itself as the voice of those voiceless babies. But pro-lifers also feel called to be the face of love for women in the difficult circumstance of an unwanted pregnancy. The most loving environment a troubled pregnant woman can find is not in a Planned Parenthood clinic, where she will be told her decision to terminate is okay, even liberating. It is within the walls of one of the crisis pregnancy centers that are now more numerous than abortion clinics.[1]

In these havens for mothers and children, a choice is offered that has no death toll: raise the child or follow the path of adoption. Clients are assured that if they choose to raise their babies, they will receive both material and spiritual help. The notion that discarding a life is somehow better than "bringing an unwanted child into the world" reflects a false choice. If a mother feels unable to keep and raise her child, adoption allows her baby to live and be cared for by parents who *do* want it.

When a troubled mother chooses life, the rewards multiply. She lives unburdened by a decision she could well regret forever, adoptive parents get the joy of a child they would not have otherwise, and most important of all, a child lives that would otherwise die.

Denying the humanity of the unborn child allows pro-choicers to avoid the terrible truth about abortion, but future generations may view today's prenatal extermination with the same horror with which we look back on slavery.

The Constitution protects the right to terminate pregnancy.

Try looking for it.

In January 1973, the Supreme Court invented a federal right to terminate a pregnancy. Intent on freeing women from the claims of their unborn children but lacking any grounds for doing so in the text of the Constitution, the Court made use of a line of egregiously mis-reasoned cases from the 1960s to reach its desired conclusion, setting the stage for the judicial tyranny that has stained every decade since.

Justice Harry Blackmun's capricious majority opinion in *Roe v. Wade* relies on the right to "privacy," which the Warren Court, striking down a state restriction on birth control, had concocted in *Griswold v. Connecticut* (1965). Con Law 101: If the Constitution does not forbid laws against something, the people may outlaw it. Your religion, your speech, and, yes, your gun cannot be outlawed. But if the citizens of a city, a state, or the nation at large choose to outlaw tricycles, cucumbers, or contraceptives, they may do so. You may consider such laws absurd, which is why they are so uncommon, but "absurd" does not equal "unconstitutional."

If the people of Connecticut, acting through their representatives, wanted to say no IUDs or condoms for anyone, that was their will and that should have been that. The solution was for those who disagreed to demand legislation to the contrary (which, in the mid-1960s, would have happened in very short order if the law was being enforced, which it wasn't).

State-by-state solutions are how abortion should be handled as well. Overturning *Roe v. Wade* would not establish a constitutional right to life from the moment of conception. It would simply return the issue to where the Ninth and Tenth Amendments require it to be settled—the states. A state wishing to retain permissive abortion laws could do so, and the state next door that wished to curtail the practice could do so as well.

This sensible solution to one of our most volatile issues is impossible until the horrendous *Roe* decision is overturned. When that happens, it will not be the work of pro-life justices forcing their will on the minority; it will be the work of justices who recognize that abortion rights are not addressed in the Constitution and are to be settled as the Bill of Rights requires.

Abortion restrictions must contain exceptions for rape and incest.

Fearful of appearing "unreasonable," some conservatives soften their anti-abortion stance by making sure no one thinks they would deny an abortion to the victim of rape or incest. At a shallow level, this position may draw a nod of approval. Our natural sympathy with the victim of such a horrible crime, whose pregnancy is not the result of a choice she made, makes the denial of abortion in cases of rape or incest seem draconian. On the campaign trail, many of the most pro-life Republicans get tongue-tied when asked if the crimes of rape and incest should be followed by the additional tragedy of abortion.

So here's the hard truth. Innocent unborn life is either sacred or it is not. If it is, neither rape nor incest changes that in the least. There are many people whose lives are the product of these terrible crimes, and those lives are no less precious or worthy of protection under law. A human life is a human life.

You can't carve out a rape or incest exception and say with the next breath that unborn life is sacred. If it is not, women may terminate pregnancies for rape or incest—or pretty much any other reason they like. Why? Because to the baby, it does not matter. A child snuffed out because of the circumstances in which it was conceived is no less dead than the child snuffed out because its mother did not wish to be bothered. There's a name for people who would allow abortion in the case of rape or incest: pro-choice. Narrowly so, but pro-choice nonetheless.

Professing pro-life credentials with an asterisk for rape or incest is morally incoherent. If you assert that unborn life is sacred, there can be no rape or incest exception. If you seek that exception, you are not fundamentally pro-life.

A victim of rape or incest who has to bear the child of her attacker should experience the embrace of loving support—and there are numerous places where that support can be found—and she should have the option of entrusting the child to loving adoptive parents if she so chooses.

I have spoken to people who were conceived by rape and incest. Few of them have been raised by their birth mothers, but all are grateful beyond words that those mothers allowed them to come into the world.

Pro-lifers are against "women's health."

There are few rhetorical tricks as pervasive as the sugarcoating of abortion services as "women's health." Conflating abortion with breast cancer screenings and other medical services, the abortion lobby accuses pro-lifers of joining the so-called "War on Women." But no one seeks to disturb Planned Parenthood or any other institution in the provision of nonlethal services. If those clinics want to offer mammograms or cholesterol screenings or knitting classes, there will be no protesters outside their doors.

Much is made of Planned Parenthood's claim that the 330,000 abortions it commits each year account for only 3 percent of its business. If that's true, then why doesn't it avoid the controversy and limit itself to activities that don't kill anyone? The reason is that abortion is a sacrament to them. And the 3 percent figure is a fraud. *National Review* editor Rich Lowry explains:

> By Planned Parenthood's math, a woman who gets an abortion but also a pregnancy test, an STD test and some contraceptives has received four services, and only 25 percent of them are abortion. This is a little like performing an abortion and giving a woman an aspirin, and saying only half of what you do is abortion.
>
> Such cracked reasoning could be used to obscure the purpose of any organization. The sponsors of the New York City Marathon could count each small cup of water they hand out (some 2 million cups, compared with

45,000 runners) and say they are mainly in the hydration business.[2]

Abortion clinics want the public to think of them as health care facilities, but they don't want the government to treat them like health care facilities. For instance, when the State of Texas imposed new safety regulations on abortion clinics, the clinics howled that low-income women's health care was at risk. It did not take long to discern that this was complete bunk. The website healthytexaswomen.org directs women of modest means to an array of services that the abortion industry would have them believe only they provide: breast and cervical cancer screening, pregnancy testing, treatment of sexually-transmitted diseases, mental health counseling, family violence resources, even help to stop smoking. These services are provided at little or no cost in a manner any liberal should love: through state government.

The pro-life threat to "women's health" is a ruse. It's all about abortion, that deadly guarantor of consequence-free sex.

Euthanasia is "death with dignity."

There's more to life than birth, of course. Many pro-lifers are as concerned about the growing taste for euthanasia and physician-assisted suicide as they are about abortion.

Various states have passed measures offering options to patients facing daunting declines in health on the way to a possibly painful or debilitating death. At a purely surface level, the demand is easy to understand. If one faces a terminal illness with a long, excruciating decline, why not just skip that burden and take the exit ramp now?

The thing is, there is an answer to that question.

The logic against a self-chosen departure date relies on the understanding that our lives are not our property, but rather a gift from God that we are not free to discard. Pastors also teach that suffering has a purpose that may not be apparent to the patient or his family, but that a decision to end life on human timing rather than God's is a sin as well as a danger to society. Proponents of so-called "death with dignity" statutes will properly argue that these objections are a matter of religious belief, which the state is not entitled to impose on individuals. True enough. So we need an argument that is compelling irrespective of personal faith.

As a purely practical matter, how bad off does someone need to be before we consider killing him or letting him kill himself? Immobilized patients unable to speak or care for themselves but nonetheless likely to remain alive indefinitely seem to be easy cases. But in the bizarre 1990s cases of Dr. Jack Kevorkian, I remember the filmed testimony of patients who were thrilled to have his "help" in bringing their unwanted lives to a close. The problem was, they were sitting upright, unremarkably sipping coffee with functional hands, speaking with working mouths. So where is the bar supposed to be set? At some level of disability, or just on the whim of thoroughly functional patients?

Investigative reporting found that some of Kevorkian's "patients" were not terminally ill, that others were not suffering particularly serious pain, and that still others seemed to have emotional problems. This is a master class in the profound mess that can occur if we push forward obsessed with the "right to die."

In 2014, Brittany Maynard of California took her own life with medical help in Oregon under that state's "Death with Dignity" law. Diagnosed with brain cancer and given six months to live in April of that year, she had already outlived that deadline when she ended her life in November. Her death certificate is a lie. Oregon law allowed it to say brain cancer when in reality she committed suicide with an overdose of barbiturates, closing the door on any possibility of the kind of miracles that do sometimes happen.

The popular culture is not helpful. The romance novel *Me Before You*, brought to the screen in 2016, is designed to make us cheer a disabled man's decision to end his life rather than face disability. A woman introduced to our hero for the purpose of persuading him to live is caught up in the sheer poetic beauty of coming around to his way of thinking—that his is a life not worth living. For the umpteenth time: thanks, Hollywood. This is a fictional tale, of course, and writers may crank out whatever they like. But in clearly goading us to follow our own utilitarian logic instead of revering life as a gift from God, the message of *Me Before You* is really "us before Him."

Again, states wishing to adopt a cavalier attitude toward human life are free to do so. But let's not obscure what's going on by calling it "death with dignity." If you're looking for dignity, consider the stories of people whose strong faith has seen them to a natural end. Those stories are sometimes fraught with challenges and pain, but they also reveal the satisfaction and peace that are the fruit of subjugating our will to God's. There are countless cases of people given news of impending death who make the most of life not by ending it on an impulse but by wringing out every drop of joy and purpose that they can, inspiring countless others in the process.

That may not be a choice we can force on the unwilling, but if citizens are helped to appreciate both life's meaning and the slippery slope before us, America's regard for life will be enriched.

9

HATE

America is a racist nation.

One hundred fifty years after the Civil War and a half-century after the Civil Rights Act, can racism still be found in America? Of course. Racism is an ugly human trait that will persist in some residual form even after it has been purged from laws and institutions.

Historically, racism in America was primarily about white people oppressing black people. But in the multicultural twenty-first century, everyone has been freed to harbor racial animosity against everyone else. If "racism" is the mistreatment or denigration of persons solely because of their race, then it is by no means limited to white antagonism toward blacks.

The only remaining racism actually enshrined in American law and public policy is affirmative action, an embodiment of white guilt that condescendingly lowers standards for minorities in education and employment. Race relations will be immeasurably improved when no one's presence in a particular school, university, or job can be implicitly attributed to ethnicity.

Racial preferences are either right or wrong. If they are wrong, as we have been taught for several generations now, they do not become right when wielded as instruments of revenge. Oprah Winfrey, born in Mississippi in the 1950s, knows a thing or two about overcoming prejudice. One of the foremost American success stories gave us some of the greatest wisdom on this subject when she said she "was raised to believe that excellence is the best deterrent to racism."

Compare this attitude with the lessons delivered daily to young African Americans by activists peddling the lie that their main challenges are bigotry and white privilege. Of course there are vestiges of racism that yield the occasional injustice, but they have been chased into the darkest corners of society. Just a couple of generations after the governor of Alabama defiantly promised "Segregation forever!" one of the worst things you can be called in America is a racist. The mere whiff of it can ruin a reputation and a career. This shift took place with head-spinning speed.

People who believe that racial attitudes have scarcely budged since the fifties may be under the spell of politicians and activists who promise that the government can deliver them from this manufactured plight. Bold steps were necessary in the era of Rosa Parks and Martin Luther King Jr. to purge America of the legal and institutional injustices that had afflicted blacks since they arrived on slave ships. Today, however, racial tensions can be resolved through interpersonal relationships in an atmosphere of enlightenment and decency.

When former Attorney General Eric Holder condemned the United States as a "nation of cowards" in need of a "national conversation" about race, race relations deteriorated before our eyes. The only "conversations" that grievance-mongers like Holder and, sadly, our first president of color are interested in are those that conform to their narrative of an America mired in racism from which only they can extract it. The fact is that the American conversation about race takes place every day as people of every race interact civilly with each other, adding year after year to the reservoir of maturity and good-will.

The occasional outburst from a white racist is a historical hiccup. Far more prevalent these days are poisonous movements like Black Lives Matter, a hate group that throws kerosene on the embers of our racial stresses. Accusations of racism against advocates of a strong border or those who take seriously the threat of global jihad likewise undermine racial and ethnic harmony. False accusations like these trivialize a serious social evil that genuine heroes have struggled to eradicate. Their successes are dishonored by today's false and reflex-ive cries of racism.

Strong immigration laws are anti-Hispanic.

I have always thought that U.S. citizens of Hispanic descent should be the loudest voices against illegal immigration. After all, what harms the reputation of the hard-working legal immigrant more than guilt by association with the millions of illegal intruders from Latin America?

The problem extends far beyond Hispanic populations, of course, but the signature immigration challenge of our time is the influx from south of our border with Mexico. These millions of illegal arrivals are a burden on our nation's resources and a threat to our public safety. Not every "undocumented" alien is a drain on our welfare state or a career criminal, but our laws should be respected on principle. When they are flouted for decades, the damage is not just to our economy but to our national spirit.

We are a nation made great by millions of immigrants—legal ones. Yet that distinction is lost when concern about illegal immigration is slanderously labeled "anti-immigrant."

Compounding this dishonesty is the misrepresentation of standing for strong borders as a sign of antipathy for Hispanics. One of the best ways to bask in love at a Tea Party rally is to reveal yourself as a legal immigrant. Opponents of illegal immigration aren't displaying racial hang-ups, they're objecting to behavior. Obey the law in coming to America, and the staunchest border warrior will offer a welcoming hand.

So why do so many law-abiding Hispanic Americans oppose strong borders that would improve their quality of life? Do they wish to see the Latino population swell for political or cultural reasons?

And why do so many vote against Republicans who share their social conservatism? I have heard forever that conservative rhetoric just seems "hostile." If so, we need better communicators. There is no aversion to Hispanics in the simple wish for an America that gets control over who gets in.

Conservatism wages a "War on Women."

The funny thing about the supposed "War on Women" is that you never hear conservative women complain about it. Might this suggest that the battle is based on politics and not sex?

In one of its manifold offenses against the language, the Left argues that laws promoting reproductive morality are somehow an affront to womanhood. That takes some nerve. Conservative women defend the unborn, issuing not one complaint about being targeted for warfare. The "War on Women" is in fact a ruse to avoid an actual discussion of the issues. A quick tour of the areas where conservatism is supposedly a pit of misogyny:

- All reproductive matters, of course. Stick up for babies in the womb and you hate women. Display a moral objection to contraception (as millions of observant Catholics do), and you hate women.
- Violence against women. Conservative skepticism of "rape culture" reflects not a lack of evidence but a stunning insensitivity, and thus a hatred of women.
- Equal pay for equal work. Failure to swallow the lie that women make seventy-eight cents (or whatever is the figure du jour) for every dollar that men make for the same work is a sure sign of being a woman-hater.

In each charge, facts are set aside in favor of an ad hominem attack. Since millions of Americans pay wafer-thin attention to the realities behind such slanders, they are unaware of why any decent human being would oppose things that are "pro-woman."

Maybe it's a better idea to be pro-truth.

The truth is that Americans occupy a wide spectrum of opinion on abortion and birth control. Men and women are found at every point along that spectrum. Women skew more liberal than men, but the millions of women with conservative views on reproductive morality hold those views for the same reasons men do.

No one is ambivalent about the horrors of rape. But a strain of virulent feminism has cooked up the notion of pockets of "rape culture"—places where rape is common, and met with nonchalance. The combination of an absurdly broad definition of sexual assault with the sexual license that liberals promote on college campuses and elsewhere is a recipe for a witch hunt. Pushing back against such fraud is not a sign of ambivalence about rape, it is a quest for accuracy. And as for the notion that our revulsion toward rape is dwindling, ask Bill Cosby if he thinks America has grown ambivalent about the issue.

Finally, women make less per capita than men because they move in and out of the workplace to get married, have children, and pursue other interests—especially if they're blessed to live with one of those dinosaurs, the Breadwinner Husband. There is virtually no wage gap for women who launch into a career and avoid detours (which often means not getting married).[1] There are also more men than women in the college majors that tend to lead to high pay.

The "War on Women" crowd knows that facts and logic are not on their side, nor are millions of Americans, many of them actual women. So they trowel out these attacks on their opponents, rewarded with the nodding agreement of the inattentive.

The good news is that majorities of both sexes spot this nonsense as political posturing,[2] recognizing that most arguments about sex are not about manhood or womanhood but about politics.

The Confederate flag represents hate, but Black Lives Matter does not.

When twenty-one-year-old Dylann Roof opened fire on a prayer meeting at a black church in Charleston, South Carolina, in June 2015, establishing racial hatred as his motivation was simple. He actually confessed that his goal was to spark a race war. It was a triumph of the human spirit when family members of the victims attended his bond hearing, not to shower him with vengeful wrath (which he surely deserved), but to speak of mercy and forgiveness.

Roof's affinity for Confederate symbols sealed the diagnosis of bigotry, sparking a wave of activism that led to the Confederate flag's removal from the South Carolina statehouse grounds. There is no doubt that such imagery is a favored fetish of racists. But does that mean that everyone with a Confederate license plate bracket is wistful about the good old days of slavery?

Over the course of countless radio talk-show conversations on this subject, I have hammered out what I think is a reasonable truce: Confederate flag devotees should acknowledge that the symbol represents a regime that enslaved the ancestors of black Americans, and while it is not necessarily evidence of racism today, there are plenty of racists who embrace it. In return, Confederate flag critics should acknowledge that not everyone in a Lynyrd Skynyrd T-shirt thinks the wrong side won the Civil War.

Every drop of my blood is of Southern extraction, but I don't give a flip about Confederate symbols. I will neither emulate nor condemn those who have flags hanging in the den. Nor do I begrudge African American distaste for it. The black men and women of modern America can be forgiven for seeing the Confederate flag less as a symbol of states' rights than as the emblem beneath which their ancestors were whipped.

For that reason, I've never opposed removing Confederate symbols from state flags or government property, places where the symbols of a state should have a uniting effect. But it's just wrong to presume that every display of a Confederate flag is evidence of racism. I don't have many friends or relatives demonstrably fond of Confederate symbols, but of those who are, not one is a bigot.

In an era of contrived racial offenses, like the flap over the name of the Washington Redskins, the culture is quick to point an accusing finger at the first evidence of insufficient enlightenment. Trouble is, the assessments of such attitudes are skewed.

Take the venom spewed by Black Lives Matter, a group wrapping itself in the noble history of the civil rights movement. Emerging after the shooting of Trayvon Martin in 2012, and fueled in 2014 by the shooting of Michael Brown in Ferguson, Missouri, and the death of Eric Garner after his arrest in Staten Island, Black Lives Matter would like to be seen as vigilant watchdogs seeking police accountability.

All decent people want police accountability, especially the good cops who constitute nearly the entire force in every city. From its very name to its slanderous overgeneralizations, Black Lives Matter is an attack on policing. Their words and tactics would be easily identified as hate if they were aimed at a particular race or religion.

Take the title. "Black Lives Matter" presumes that there are legions of people, presumably in uniform, who believe that the lives of blacks do not in fact matter. This is a lie. If a group wishes to assert that black suspects have been mistreated by the police, there are examples they can point to, such as the shootings of Walter Scott in North Charleston, South Carolina, and Laquan McDonald in Chicago. But BLM's contention that the police have declared open season on young black men is simply unsupportable.

BLM is not shy about adopting the language of the most virulent haters. Marching at the Minnesota State Fair in August 2015, marchers—escorted by police officers—chanted "Pigs in a blanket, fry 'em like bacon!" This is not a quest for accountability. This is cop-hating. I'd wager there are more guys in Confederate flag shirts and baseball caps who have no quarrel with black people than there are Black Lives Matter members who are even-handed about the police.

Hate has a meaning. It is baseless hostility toward people because of what they are. But today, the label is wielded as a political weapon, as when differing beliefs are misidentified as hate. Similarly, real hate is often sugarcoated if it aligns with a progressive agenda.

Opposition to gay rights is homophobia.

Ever heard of the "Overton window"? First articulated by the late Joseph Overton of the Mackinac Center for Public Policy, it describes the range of ideas that society will tolerate at a given moment. The window comprises a spectrum of ideas from the radical, to the acceptable, to the popular, and finally those adopted as policy. Once-unthinkable ideas (voting rights for blacks, for example) may move into the window, while once-accepted ideas (slavery, for example) may become unthinkable and move out of it.

Few ideas have streaked across that spectrum with the speed of gay rights. With a little help from the Supreme Court, same-sex marriage has taken its place in the very center of the window as "policy." Yet millions of Americans hold theological or philosophical objections to homosexuality. What are we to think of them?

We know what gay-rights advocates think of them: they're haters. But is this fair?

Let's stipulate that there is indeed such a thing as homophobia, an aversion to gays simply for being gay, with hostility manifested in cruel speech, discrimination, and sometimes physical attacks. But does belief in biblical teaching about sexual behavior belong in the same category? Scripture teaches that homosexual acts are sinful, but it also commands us to love the sinner, and for the most part that's what Christians do.

But people of faith are told they cannot love homosexuals without approving of homosexuality. The failure to embrace, even celebrate, gayness is just another earnestly held belief that the Left chalks up as hate.

The problem is that this nonsense is not just a matter of personal opinion; it is spreading into the law. From the Boy Scouts of America to local bakers and florists who decline to participate in gay weddings, court cases and penalties are in store for Americans who insist on adhering to natural law and biblical morality. Traditionalists are chided for being "on the wrong side of history," but at no time in history has any major faith embraced homosexuality. This doesn't mean attitudes cannot change, but those calling for change cannot suggest that they have some preponderance of moral evidence on their side.

This debate will not be settled anytime soon. But something is wrong when peaceful and conscientious disagreement is branded as "hate," a charge calculated to delegitimize and punish dissent.

10

RELIGION

Christians are intolerant.

At the root of every stereotype is some degree of truth. There actually are Italians in the Mafia, video gamers who rarely see sunshine, and Christians who are intolerant.

But how much of Christian "intolerance" is simply people of faith making value judgments they have every right to make? The spreading anti-Christian mindset wants to marginalize believers as cruelly judgmental for their scriptural views on sexuality, human behavior, and popular culture.

Civilized society refuses to tolerate a long list of things. Some of them we make illegal—domestic violence, pedophilia, and fraud, for instance. Others are merely met with opprobrium—flag burning, fattening your kids on years of junk food, failure to recycle.

Taking any position in a political or moral argument can be viewed as intolerance. Pro-lifers are intolerant of pro-choicers and vice versa. Pacifists are intolerant of war hawks and receive intolerance in return. The air on college campuses is thick with intolerance for conservatives. Intolerance is often nothing more than disagreement.

So consider the millions who believe that the Bible is the word of God and thus not to be trifled with. Are they not allowed to believe that certain acts are forbidden by the Lord himself? And if they share this belief with others, is it proper to identify this "intolerance" as a character flaw?

Declaring to perfect strangers that they are in danger of hellfire is a breach of etiquette, but the courteous communication of values thoughtfully embraced deserves our respect. Still, some values receive more respect than others. If you get your back up about carbon footprints, Indian mascots, and the existence of rich people, you'll be applauded for your enlightened views. But if you find fault with abortion, homosexuality, adultery, and a host of other sins, you'll be singled out for abuse. Why is that? It's because demonization avoids the obligation to debate. If evangelicals are haters, they scarcely deserve a place at the table of rational discourse. The alternative is actually having to defend the things Christianity advises against, and that can get tricky.

There are thoughtful critics of Christianity, but all too often they can't resist the temptation to marginalize Christian views as primitive and loathsome. Christians are indeed "intolerant" of things that violate their core beliefs. So is everyone else. But no one deserves to be tagged as an unthinking dogmatist simply because the source of his assertions is his faith.

Atheism is more rational than belief in God.

Conservatives are supposed to loathe Bill Maher, and I take my share of exception when he attacks my politics or my faith. But I give him this: he is never boring and sometimes unpredictable, as when he complains that the Left does not take global jihad seriously. Maybe his clarity on Islam is the product of a sliver of rationality, or perhaps it's just part of a broader hatred of all religion. Maher is an inveterate mocker of religious belief in general. Stephen Colbert once gamely tried to lure him back to the Catholic faith in which both were raised. "Admit there are things greater than you in the universe that you do not understand," he coaxed. Maher's rejoinder: "I do admit there are things in the universe I don't understand, but my response to that is not to make up silly stories."

Silly stories. The invisible man in the sky. Fables made up by man to force-feed the concept of God. Such are the stones cast by atheists, as if their position does not require an enormous leap of faith itself.

Let us stipulate that most people of faith believe in a supernatural God whom they cannot see. In the case of Christians, they believe that God became man in the womb of a virgin, emerged from obscurity in Galilee to preach and work miracles, died on a cross, and then rose from the dead so that our sins can be forgiven. That's a lot to swallow. Much of the story is beyond the reach of scientific inquiry. But does logic dictate that nothing exists beyond the observable, material, humanly graspable world?

Is a godless explanation of the cosmos any less fanciful than the book of Genesis? The secular story is that man exists because Enzyme A bumped into Enzyme B in some primordial soup eons ago. An admittedly complex chain of events ensued, leading eventually to you and me. In the purely material account, if one variable had been changed, none of us would have been born. People of faith find it difficult if not impossible to consider that our lives are the product of a wholly random succession of fortunate moments orchestrated by no one.

So consider that both the believer and the atheist come to the table with answers that require a certain type of faith. The religious faith is based on a decision to believe that there is a Supreme Being, an intelligent creator. The godless faith is that this all happened by itself. Since neither side can definitively prove itself to the other, both are left with assumptions based on what makes sense to them. Each side thinks it is right and the other side is mistaken. But there is no logic that suggests the atheist is somehow more sensible. The atheist looks at the vastness of the universe, the wonders of our earth, and the mystery of our very existence and concludes that no one is behind them. How is this more reasonable than my belief that it is all the work of a God who exists beyond our meager perceptions?

The debate between believers and non-believers is always lively but almost always fairly useless, both sides affirming, in essence, "I believe what I believe because it is what I believe." Not much common ground to strive for there, and no problem in both sides holding to their beliefs for reasons that feel self-evident. But let's dispense with the insult that the non-believers deserve some gold star for limiting their conclusions to evidence they can see.

Islam is a religion of peace.

I am grateful every day for both presidential terms of George W. Bush. I was not a fan of the bailouts or No Child Left Behind or a two-state "solution" involving Israel and the Palestinians, but I know my family was kept safer by the war taken straight into the gut of the part of the world that wants us dead.

By the time Barack Obama leaves office, we will have endured the dangers of failing to fight the war that jihadists have never stopped fighting against us. If Bush's successor had maintained or even ramped up the war footing that brought Iraq to the brink of functionality, who knows? We might not be playing whack-a-mole with ISIS today.

But even as he steeled the nation for the launch of a war on terror, President Bush could not avoid stepping for a moment into the trap that has hindered our fight against this enemy—the political correctness that prods so many to understate the jihadist ideology that permeates much of the Islamic world.

Before the dust at Ground Zero had settled, Americans knew that all of Islam was not to blame for the 9/11 attacks. But every jihadist is motivated by Islam. President Bush had the strength of will to take the war to the enemy, but the week after 9/11, he bowed to PC pressures. Speaking in Washington to an audience of Muslim clergymen who expressed a shared revulsion at the attacks, the president declared, "The face of terror is not the true faith of Islam. That's not what Islam is all about. Islam is peace."[1]

While he did not repeat the common error that the name Islam means "peace" (it means submission to Allah), Bush nevertheless denied the true nature of what had happened a few days earlier. While responsibility for 9/11 should not be attributed to every Muslim, no one, especially an American president, should fail to appreciate the extent of the approval for terrorist acts in the Muslim world.

The terror campaigns of al Qaeda and ISIS since 2001 make it clear that jihadists command an extensive following among the world's Muslims. The Pew Research Center famously found in 2006 that while support for violence against civilians "to defend Islam" had begun to wane since 2002, more than 50 percent of those polled in Jordan, supposedly an American ally, still approved.[2] In Lebanon, not known as a hotbed of jihad, 39 percent offered a nod of the head to terror. One can only imagine what the figures might have been in Iraq, Afghanistan, or Syria, where collecting such data might get a researcher blown to bits.

Islam's apologists point to Koranic texts condemning acts of evil and specifically proscribing violence against the innocent. But therein lies the problem. To more Muslims than we would like to know, the infidels—Christians, Jews, Americans, Israelis—are not "innocent." We are guilty of the most punishable of blasphemies: resistance to the spread of the caliphate. In the eyes of imams the world over, including growing portions of the West, lopping our heads off or flying planes into our buildings is not evil, it is justified.

What was true on September 11, 2001, is true today: some Muslims want to kill us, some don't. The entire faith does not bear the stain of jihadism, but it is ridiculous—and dangerous—to pretend that radicals are merely a splinter group. In fact, we should revisit the meaning of "radical," in the sense of departure from a norm. The mass murderers of 9/11, of *Charlie Hebdo*, of San Bernardino, of Brussels, and of Orlando were not deviants from Koranic tradition. They were true believers, following in the violent tradition of fourteen centuries. The "radicals" are actually the modern Muslims seeking to distance themselves from their faith's bloody legacy.

There is a civil war within Islam, and we'd better hope the good guys win. But we do not hasten that day by denying who the bad guys are, how many of them there are, or how many fans they have.

A religion deserves to be judged by what its leaders teach and what its followers do. Twenty-first-century Islam offers at best a mixed picture, neither wholly terrorist nor sufficiently peaceful. When terror is expunged from the teachings and practices of Islam, we can revisit its claim to be a "religion of peace."

Jesus was a liberal.

When liberals grow weary of defending the merits of their agenda, they will occasionally assert that Jesus himself is on their side, counting the Savior as a fan of massive government social spending, an enemy of the death penalty and personal wealth, and an ardent pacifist.

One problem: none of this is biblical.

Christ as a big-government advocate is the easiest of these claims to bat away. Jesus spoke often of generosity to those in need, but he never suggested that it should be disbursed in the most inefficient manner possible—through government. In fact, government doesn't just slow the process of charity, it subverts it. Charity is personal: I direct a portion of my money to destinations of my choice in order to follow the biblical calling for benevolence toward those less fortunate. When the government commandeers my money to disburse as it sees fit, that's not charity, that's redistribution. Whether to erect an all-enveloping welfare state is a prudential judgment left to the wisdom of men. No one should misrepresent Jesus by suggesting that he commands it.

To be fair, Democrats aren't the only ones asserting divine authority for their policies. Among the factors hobbling John Kasich's 2016 presidential campaign was his decision to cooperate with Obamacare by expanding Medicaid in Ohio. When challenged, he sanctimoniously defended that policy as an indicator of "how we treat the poor,"[3] echoing a lecture he delivered in 2013 to an Ohio lawmaker who dared to suggest that Medicaid was a flawed tool for actually helping people in the long term. "Now, when you die and get to the meeting with St. Peter," he told the legislator, "he's probably not going to ask you much about what you did about keeping government small. But he is going to ask you what you did for the poor. You better have a good answer."[4] The "good answer," of course, would be a lifetime of genuine charity and kindness, not complicity in the institutionalization of such personal responsibilities.

When it comes to the death penalty, opponents think their biblical case is open and shut: "Thou shalt not kill," right?

Wrong.

An attentive translation of the shortest of the Ten Commandments reveals that the original text does not refer to killing in general, but to murder. The Bible is full of righteous killing, the types that are justified today, such as just wars and self-protection. There is no blanket disapproval of killing.

As for the death penalty specifically, it is all over the Bible's pages, as far back as Genesis 9:6: "Whoever sheds man's blood, his blood will be shed by man." And for those who are fond of suggesting that Jesus hits a big reset button in the New Testament, there is no pronouncement of his that suggests the biblical precept of a death penalty is to be set aside. The Gospel of John contains the famous story of Christ's restraining a mob from stoning an adulterous woman, but this is a call for tempering justice with mercy and restraint. "Let any one of you who is without sin cast the first stone," Jesus instructs. If this were a universal commandment against such punishments, no one would ever be punished by anyone for anything, since no one is without sin.

Nor is there evidence that Jesus frowned on the wealthy. The Savior was not some Nazarene Bernie Sanders, decrying the mere existence of wealth in the hands of those who had earned it. Personal wealth is one of the potential benefits of God's favor. Yet it is a central principle of modern liberalism that private wealth is undeserved and that a collectivist government must funnel it to the less fortunate. This principle is found nowhere in the Bible.

Jesus does warn that material wealth is fleeting. "Thou fool," says God to the rich man in the parable, "this night thy soul shall be required of thee: then whose shall those things be, which thou hast provided?" (Luke 12:20). And in Matthew 19:24—"It is easier for a camel to go through the eye of a needle than for a rich man to enter the kingdom of God"—he assures us that earthly riches are not a golden ticket to Heaven. If that meant that riches were an automatic disqualification for eternal life, plenty of liberal heroes would have been cast into the Lake of Fire. But in the next verse the disciples ask, "Who, then, can be saved?" Jesus' answer, "With men, this is impossible; but with God all things are possible," indicates not only that salvation is God's work, not man's, but also that he does not broadly condemn our wealth.

Nor does Christ condemn war or warriors. He declared blessed the peacemakers and enjoined us to love our enemies, but he knew full well there were just and necessary wars before his time and that many would follow. Objecting to all war is moral idiocy. War gave birth to our nation, ended slavery, and stopped Hitler. As long as there is evil, war will sometimes be necessary to combat it.

This does not mean Jesus approves of all wars, but no one says that he does. In the gospels and the Acts of the Apostles, Jesus and his disciples frequently interact with soldiers and centurions, never suggesting that their chosen battles are incompatible with salvation.

If Jesus was not a liberal, was he a conservative? The political philosopher Russell Kirk identified six "canons of conservative thought," the first of which is "Belief in a transcendent order, or body of natural law, which rules society as well as conscience. Political problems, at bottom, are religious and moral problems."[5] If taking the moral law seriously makes one a conservative, then you can draw your own conclusions about the Lord's political affinities. But it is wise to remember what Abraham Lincoln said during the Civil War when asked if God was on his side: "Sir, my concern is not whether God is on our side; my greatest concern is to be on God's side, for God is always right."

11

HUMAN NATURE

Mankind is fundamentally good.

I remember hearing for the first time, when I was about eight, that mankind is not intrinsically good. This struck me as an insult to the human race. I wanted to think not only that the vast majority of people are good, but that they are naturally prone to goodness. My optimism was mistaken, of course, as the evidence of every human life demonstrates from the earliest stages.

Watch a pair of three-year-olds fighting over a toy truck in a sandbox. Without the civilizing restraint of adult supervision they would rip each other's throats out if they were able. Within a few years, without wise and loving instruction they will be drawn to bullying, gangs, drugs, crime, and all the fruits of self-indulgence, unequipped for a useful and happy adulthood. For the most part, you don't have to *do* anything to make a person turn out this way. It's a matter of *not* doing something. Well-adjusted, kind, principled adults will tell you about the guidance they received that pointed them in a proper direction.

Man's sinful nature is confirmed in the Bible, but it is readily observable by anyone. G. K. Chesterton called original sin "the only part of Christian theology which can really be proved."[1] It is self-evident that, left to our own inclinations, we will be absorbed with our own gratification and have little regard for others.

The naïve assumption that man is naturally good discounts the necessity of constant self-correction, which is the result of a regular evaluation of one's intentions and acts. An examination of conscience can be hard work, and some people have no interest in such heavy lifting. But for others, the discovery that they must actually work to be good is an inspiring call to action. Understanding the consequences of shirking that work is, of course, an added motivation.

We should do whatever makes us "happy."

My friend and fellow talk show host Dennis Prager wrote a book with the brilliant title *Happiness Is a Serious Problem*. It's a master class in understanding what happiness is, where it comes from, and why we should try to act happy even when we do not feel like it.

Too many people think of happiness as an evaluation of how gratified and entertained we are at any given moment. But you don't measure happiness like blood pressure. It's the result of a long pattern of good decisions and wise actions leading to real, not manufactured, self-esteem. It's measured by the gratitude of those we have served.

A life spent looking outwardly leaves little room for stewing in our own petty discontents. When things or people annoy us, when life takes a horrible turn, when we don't get exactly what we want, we can become petulant and bitter or we can show the resilience that comes from the attribute Prager identifies as most necessary for happiness: gratitude. You see this in television interviews with people outside their tornado-ravaged homes, grateful that they are alive, or in the soldier who has lost a leg but still lives to hold his newborn child. Opportunities for gratitude abound; all we have to do is take advantage of them.

When you face a tough choice, the most dangerous advice you can receive is "Do whatever makes you happy." A focus on short-term gratification rather than the long-term habit of doing the right thing is actually a prescription for eventual despair. The journey to happiness passes through self-denial, hard choices, and stark challenges. If our daily self-examination consists of questions like "Am I satisfied today?," "Am I entertained today?," and "Are my needs being met?," we're headed for trouble. The people who achieve true happiness are usually looking far down the road, not checking their mood rings from moment to moment.

You can't legislate morality.

We legislate morality all the time. Laws against murder, speeding, shoplifting, and a zillion other things constitute a message that "we believe these acts are so wrong that we will punish you if you do them." Sometimes our efforts to outlaw immoral behavior run afoul of the Constitution, as when certain forms of expression are targeted. Sometimes they prove to be imprudent, the cons outweighing the pros, as with Prohibition. But the charge of "legislating morality" is usually a device to deter laws someone just doesn't like.

Nevertheless, some argue that our current drug laws amount to the imposition of the morality of some against the liberties of others. This fails. I don't want drugs kept illegal because I'm looking to run other people's lives. I want them kept illegal because a stoned society is everybody's business. A better argument against drug laws is that they cause more problems than they solve—a reasonable if less than convincing position. States are free to legalize marijuana, and some have, but those seeking to maintain strict drug laws are within their rights and the realm of reason as well.

States should be equally free to restrict abortion, which would be legislating the moral precept that innocent human life must be protected. It is a trickier proposition to outlaw so-called "victimless" crimes—private transactions between consenting adults, such as gambling and prostitution. The libertarian argument in these cases is that they are the business of the participating parties and no one else. The opposing view is that permitting these things results in a societal debasement that warrants limitation. Whichever side you come down on, there is no doubt that laws based on the moral will of the people are permissible, even desirable, as long as an argument can be made that there is a legitimate public interest in the matter in question.

Prostitution involves a private contract between prostitute and client, but its legality implies a judgment by society that sex is just another service for sale. True, people often exchange sex for a nice meal or a drink or two or engage in promiscuity for free, but legalizing the sex trade will inevitably attract providers and consumers driven by unsavory, noxious, or even tragic motives.

Should the law protect people from their own bad judgment? If you have fifty bucks to blow at a blackjack table, whose business is it if you do? The answer is at the next table, where some forlorn soul has just lost his next mortgage payment or the kids' college money. Not all gambling has an immediate victim, but many lives are ruined by the inability to get a gambling habit under control. Still, when that happens, it is not the casino's fault but the gambler's, and making gambling illegal removes a form of recreation that many people enjoy with no harm to themselves or their loved ones.

Nowadays it is generally thought that sodomy laws dealt with something that was nobody else's business, and the "blue laws" that kept stores closed on Sundays went by the boards, for better or worse, as the pace of life speeded up and commerce became a 24/7 preoccupation. Opinion changes and—to return to the metaphor of the Overton window from Chapter 9—laws get defenestrated. But the common thread in our legislative tapestry is that some moral question is usually at issue. As long as the Constitution is honored, it can be the main factor or one of many in the lawmaking process.

Boys and girls are the same.

In her 2015 book about women in politics and business, *Broad Influence*, *Time*'s political correspondent Jay Newton-Small, no conservative herself, makes a point that any traditionalist will gladly affirm: Men and women are different creatures, and they act and react differently. Her argument that the disproportionately male worlds of Congress and corporate America would benefit from a higher dose of distinctly feminine traits like risk-aversion and collaboration is worthy of consideration. But the premise that men and women bring different decks of cards to the table should be taken as a foundation of human nature.

The differences are clear from the earliest stages of development. The observation that boys like trucks and girls like dolls is not some sinister sexist trope. It is evidence that boys and girls are different types of human beings, and that those differences are central to the definitions of maleness and femaleness as we mature.

Those denotations are under mighty assault today as LGBT activists and gender-normers seek to obliterate human basics for their own comfort and political advantage. But no matter how many people believe that marrying a man is the same as marrying a woman, no matter how many clumsy pronouns they may try to craft to replace the oppressive "him" and "her," biological truths will not be denied.

Are there overlaps? The occasional girl who prefers Tonka trucks to Barbies and the occasional boy who likes the Easy-Bake Oven more than Nerf rifles? Sure, and that doesn't always mean the kid is on the way to being gay (although it might). The traits of masculinity and femininity are usually found in men and women respectively, though not always completely and uniformly. Those exceptions do not disprove the rule.

The history of behavioral science is packed with findings that males and females learn differently, process differently, reason differently, adapt differently, cope differently, and interact differently. Although some have invoked those differences unreasonably—suggesting, for example, that women are unfit to lead businesses or that men are incapable of controlling their sexual urges—they are nevertheless to be celebrated, not denied, for they lay the groundwork for the complementary relationships we are wired to pursue.

The reality of sexual differences militates in favor of certain single-sex environments. Proponents of all-male and all-female education point to the benefits of learning without the unavoidable drama of sexual posturing. All-male associations, such as golf clubs, are not bastions of misogyny; they are enclaves where men can be men around men. Women also enjoy the value of associations restricted to women, as well they should.

But today, sexual differences are battle lines. Resistance to women in armed combat is denounced as sexism in spite of undeniable physical disparities. Are there examples of incredibly strong women who might be a match for a man on the battlefield? In rare instances, yes, but that does not make it a good idea. Turning the military into a proving ground for sexual equality will compromise the fitness of our combat forces. Do not doubt this. They may tell you today they won't lower the standards. Rest assured that tomorrow, with that number of women qualifying close to zero, they will be back to suggest that the standards must be made "fair," and that failure to do so will be akin to denying women the vote.

Jay Newton-Small's case for more women in government and private industry is also the case *against* women in combat. Risk-aversion and a search for common ground might have their place on Wall Street and in Washington, but they're not useful on a battlefield.

The contributions of women in all walks of life will continue to be of the highest value. Indeed, in many respects men simply can't match women. But insisting that womanhood is advanced by pretending that it's the same as manhood is an insult to womanhood. One is not superior to the other. They are meant to be different, to the eternal allure, bemusement, and ultimate benefit of both.

Gender differences do not matter.

"Gender" and "sex" have never meant the same thing. "Sex" is a matter of biology. A human being is of the male or the female sex, an identity determined at the level of his or her chromosomes. "Gender" was always a grammatical term. As Henry Fowler explained in his *Dictionary of Modern English Usage* (1926), "To talk of *persons or creatures of the masculine or feminine gender,* meaning *of the male or female sex*, is either a jocularity (permissible or not according to context) or a blunder." Linguistic purists lost that battle, however, and in recent years it has become common to use "gender" to refer to the cultural or social conventions of manhood and womanhood. Today, with those very concepts under attack, "gender" has expanded to denote how someone feels on a given day.

Gender dysphoria is nothing new. There have always been men who say they feel more like women, and vice versa. We always understood that when that happened, something had gone seriously wrong, but we treated it as a private misfortune that was no one else's business. Now we call such people "transgendered," and instead of trying to help them achieve clarity, we insist that everyone else sign into their perceptual disorder.

An appropriate desire to be kind to a small number of deeply troubled persons has mutated into a fearsome crusade—backed by the combined powers of the federal government, the media, and big business—to impose gender anarchy at every level of society. Eliminating any doubt about whether the preferences of less than 0.5 percent of the population will trump the standards and even the physical security of the other 99.5 percent, the sexual Red Guards have now ordered that everyone must have access to the public toilets and school locker rooms that correspond to his or her self-declared "gender identity."

Efforts to stop this lunacy—like the North Carolina law requiring people to use public facilities corresponding to the sex on their birth certificate—have been treated like the reincarnation of Jim Crow. News reports on National Public Radio, for example, referred to the North Carolina measure as a law to "strip" LGBT persons of their "civil rights." Goodwill and reason are impossible to find as activism consumes the oxygen.

What would a reasonable path forward look like? First, the transgendered need to know that they are not the only souls who deserve to feel "comfortable." Social contortions to accommodate the rare man who identifies as a woman should not be at the expense of millions of actual women and girls who have no interest in intimate encounters with a male in the early stages of exploring his gender identity.

We're told that this is a non-problem, that there are not hordes of she-males ready to barge into the showers with our wives and daughters. True, but there aren't hordes of thieves trying to get into my house at night, either. But I keep my doors locked because there might be just one. Sometimes it is reasonable to reduce risks to as close to zero as we can. "Bathroom bill" supporters do not need to overstate the problem to make their point. The average man who will walk into the ladies' room will not be a predator, but opening that door to every gender-explorer will certainly make misbehavior easier.

Men and women suffering from gender dysphoria need our empathy and prayers. Protecting public decency doesn't require ridiculing them or making light of their plight. Cruelty is never a good tactic.

Funny thing is, the solution is right in front of our faces in countless businesses: the one-person restroom. First devised as "family restrooms" for mothers with little boys or dads with little girls, such facilities spare the transgendered the distress of walking into a restroom they do not wish to use and spare everyone else the jolt of running into someone of the opposite sex coming out of a stall. What's not to like?

Plenty, it seems. The LGBT warriors are not interested in an "accommodation." They are intent on crushing the opposition. The "bathroom wars" are just a preview of coming attractions. Businesses are stumbling over each other in the rush to fall in line, and politicians who have no personal interest in opening the next front in the Sexual Revolution are deciding that this is not a hill they wish to die on.

What is more important than the truth about our identity as human beings? The assault on manhood and womanhood will have repercussions far beyond the question of who uses which john at Target.

Kids do not need a parent at home.

Few social changes have been as consequential as the end of the expectation that a full-time parent will be at home with the kids. Households with a stay-at-home mom dipped below 50 percent in the mid-1960s and bottomed out at 23 percent in 1999. Since then, the pendulum has swung back a little, reaching 29 percent in 2012.[2] This is not wholly due to mothers' wishing to be at home to nurture. Some of those women can't find work, others are in some type of schooling. But the vast majority of women at home with kids are there because they want to be. The problem is we don't have enough women with that priority.

But we do have a growing number of stay-at-home dads. Their numbers doubled from 1989 to 2012[3] for a variety of reasons, including unemployment and disability. But whatever the reason parents stay at home, there are impressive benefits from that decision.

There is no substitute for a loving parent at home caring for children as they grow, especially in the early years. Of course there are single mothers who do not have that option (don't ever say "luxury"), and economic factors can require both parents to work. But every morning across this country, children are dumped into day care simply so that Mom and Dad can afford life's finer things.

That's not good. And the problem is aggravated by a flood of books and articles designed to assuage the proper resulting guilt. Some of the most popular themes:

- Kids of stay-at-home parents are "clingier" than the supposedly better-adjusted kids who are used to being warehoused since infancy.
- Relationships suffer because the working parent comes home to a partner whose day has been spent in a wholly different grind, who craves relief from child care from someone who understandably just wants to unwind.
- Children cared for by nannies, babysitters, or day care workers all day benefit from having more people who love them. They are more resourceful and learn to do things for themselves. I'll bet they do; imagine how proficient the kids would be if they were raised by wolves!
- It's gratifying to be appreciated both at home and at work. So why not split the day into five or six other pursuits where we can be appreciated all over town? For parents, the appreciation that matters most is from the children we choose to bring into the world.

The spin machine is at work everywhere, taking particular aim at women who ignore the siren song of feminism and its devaluation of staying at home with the kids. Feminists will tell you they seek "choices" for women, but it's clear that the choice they favor is to leave the home and strike a blow for womankind in the workforce. They point to happy kids in households with working moms, and there are many. But no one is arguing that it is impossible to raise kids successfully when both parents work. Nevertheless, child-rearing is a full-time job that is difficult to farm out, no matter how virtuous the caregivers. Our children, and our society, are suffering from the abandonment of the expectation that kids will be cared for by the people to whom they matter most—their parents.

Diversity is a necessity.

Diversity is wonderful. Or it is a pain. It depends on whether it occurs naturally or by a battle of wills.

It is beautiful to see people of varying races, religions, and backgrounds living and working together. Everywhere I have lived and everywhere I have worked, I have been enriched by associating with people unlike me living lives unlike mine. After a childhood in the salad bowl (not quite a melting pot) of the Washington, D.C., suburbs, my later stops have put me in neighborhoods that shared a little more of my whiteness and my Christianity. But from the ethnic and religious miscellany of New York City and California to the multicultural flavors of my native Texas, I have been enriched by the marvelous variety of the people with whom I have shared life's road.

The beauty of this diversity is the fruit of the freedom from which it originates. It is wonderful when different types of people choose to live and work together. Diversity becomes less charming when engineered by force.

In today's workplaces and universities, anywhere people come together, we are told the most serious shortcoming imaginable is insufficient diversity. More specifically, the problem is usually too many white people or too many men. No one points a finger at black colleges because of a dearth of whites, and no one harasses women's clubs because there are no men in the membership. But God help the institution that lacks the minimum representation of minorities and women. If it just so happens that the right sorts of people have not chosen to work or study or recreate or live there, social engineers will bring down the heavy corrective boot.

If an environment is too white, racism is assumed, which must be extirpated by the force of law. Now if persons of color are indeed systematically excluded by reason of their race, then all good people join in decrying such bigotry. But some colleges and workplaces are disproportionately white (relative to the general population) because that's what the applicant pool or the admission requirements produced. In a truly color-blind world—supposedly our ideal—no one would care. If a school or a business wound up predominantly white, black, Asian, or Hispanic, it would be presumed that those were the people who happened to show up. But such peaceful resolution is impossible when all eyes are peeled for grievances.

Such activism has been disastrous for race relations. As affirmative action insults applicants of color by dumbing down requirements for them, the resulting presumptions create an environment no self-respecting person should desire.

Are we truly better off when it's assumed that black freshmen or new Hispanic employees are there because the standards were relaxed for them? The supposition should always be that the people around us at work and at school all arrived without race preferences. Wasn't the dream of Martin Luther King Jr. and the civil rights movement—genuine equality of opportunity?

Nowadays, our interactions are poisoned by puppet-masters enforcing certain racial proportions, even if it means dumbing down standards for some and excluding others who have met those standards. This is not a recipe for racial goodwill. Minorities are excelling in every walk of life, and we are all able to live, work, and send our kids to school wherever we wish. The shoehorning of diversity undervalues the achievement of everyone who has met color-blind standards.

Of course we remain vigilant against real racism. And of course we celebrate real diversity when it occurs in our multicultural and free society. But diversity for its own sake is not a necessity, and mandating it is actually an affront to individual dignity.

12

FIGHTING TERROR

We need to understand terrorists.

Demonstrating the kind of leadership that has not exactly sent ISIS trembling back into its caves, Secretary of State John Kerry held court at a February 2015 White House summit on "violent extremism," the absurdly cleansed term the Obama administration uses because it cannot speak the name of the real enemy, the jihadist wing of Islam.

He offered up the usual list of phony reasons why people are flocking to join terrorist groups: discrimination, oppression, and my favorite, "rebellion against anonymity." History is replete with groups who have been oppressed, discriminated against, and cast into the abyss of "anonymity," whatever that is. I don't recall a tendency of any of them to respond by exterminating as many innocents as they could.

The secretary's explanations betrayed a concern too common among Western leaders. As he told his audience, "You cannot defeat what you don't understand." Really? I'm not so sure. Do we need to fully grasp the murky motives of the 9/11 hijackers and those who have followed to stop them?

Of course we try to understand what drives wrongdoing of every type, from individual criminals, to hordes of rioters, to waves of terrorists. Such knowledge may help us prevent the next heinous attack. But when the John Kerrys of the world talk about *understanding* terrorists, they call to mind the French proverb "To understand all is to forgive all," which is a poor prescription for fighting terrorists.

This instinct to over-analyze terrorists drove Kerry's foot into his mouth after the November 2015 terror attacks in Paris. Comparing that slaughter with the Charlie Hebdo massacre of the previous January, he mused, "There's something different about what happened from *Charlie Hebdo*, and I think everybody would feel that…. There was a sort of particularized focus and perhaps even a legitimacy in terms of—not a legitimacy, but a rationale that you could attach yourself to somehow and say, okay, they're really angry because of this and that."

Might we conclude that the proper government reaction to mass murder is not to speculate why the killers are "really angry" but to hunt them down and stop them?

It is hard, I admit, to look at a wide swath of humanity and conclude that it is so twisted by evil that it must be destroyed. But we did it in two world wars. Did our victory over Hitler require us to "understand" the Third Reich? It did not. It required the military might necessary to pulverize it. Who can truly understand what drives jihadists to slaughter the innocent? Such analysis is a worthy enough philosophical exercise, but it should not distract those whose duty is to protect us.

Criticizing jihad is Islamophobic.

A "Council on American-Islamic Relations" sounds like a great idea. If there is anything we need, it is an honest and substantive discourse on the relations of this free nation with the adherents of Islam—those who have assimilated American values and those who have not, including the substantial number who would like to kill us. There is in fact an organization with that name, but while it pays lip service to the cause of peace, CAIR is most often heard from when non-Muslims express concern about Islam's dark side. It is quick to denounce vigilance against terrorism as Islamophobia and concern about waves of young male Middle Eastern refugees as racist. CAIR sees the United States as a cauldron of anti-Muslim hate, even though Americans' restraint after 9/11 and the succeeding jihadist attacks should fill the rest of the world with wonder. The widespread attacks on Muslims that would have followed as a matter of course in most times and places never happened here.

Jews are the targets of more religiously-motivated hate crimes, per capita, than Muslims are.[1] Though there is no evidence that Muslims in America face a disproportionate threat to their safety or welfare, CAIR finds an Islamophobe under every rock. Remember that a phobia is an *unreasonable* fear or disdain. Overgeneralizations about Muslim involvement with terrorism are properly dismissed in our exceedingly decent society, but apprehensions about spreading jihadism are not unreasonable.

Objections to unvetted Muslim immigration draw bipartisan fire. Democrats reflexively denounce such watchfulness as bigotry, and some Republicans join them, either because they genuinely share that indefensible opinion or because they fear that toughness on the issue may cost votes.

South Carolina Governor Nikki Haley, delivering the Republican response to Obama's final State of the Union speech, scolded those who do not share her nonchalance about Muslim immigration: "During anxious times, it can be tempting to follow the siren call of the angriest voices. We must resist that temptation." This was a slap in the face to the frontrunners in her party's presidential contest at the time, Donald Trump and Ted Cruz. It was the first time I could recall Democrats and Republicans crafting the same enemies list.

Taking credible threats to national security seriously is not "anger" but prudence. But ask yourself—would some righteous anger be so unreasonable? It might suggest that what is threatened—our country and our way of life—is precious.

Fears of sharia law are unfounded.

Opinions vary on where vigilance against Muslim extremism actually becomes Islamophobia. Similarly, it is hard to pin down the moment when it is wise to become concerned about the priming of America for an influx of sharia law. Many European nations see pockets of it already. The election of a Muslim mayor of London in May 2016 does not mean that sharia courts will be setting up in the halls of the Old Bailey, and no one expects the Constitution to give way to a new caliphate in the near term. But such developments are often unnoticed until they are irreversible.

As Middle Eastern immigrants have cascaded into Europe, its major cities have been transformed. Mass Muslim migration does not deliver an automatic hit to the quality of life, but in observable ways,

European capitals are taking on shades of Arab-world metropolitan life in ways that are not always charming. America is not immune. Nearly a decade ago, an editorial in *Investor's Business Daily* noted the changes in the Virginia suburbs of Washington, D.C.:

> In Baileys Crossroads, skinned goats are delivered daily to several halal butcher shops located in shopping centers where all the signs are in Arabic. Women shop in head-to-toe black abayas. You'd never know this is a suburb of the nation's capital. Concerned longtime residents have seen it turn into "Northern Virginiastan."
>
> The pundits who mouth pleasant platitudes about American Muslims being more "integrated" have never spent much time in Northern Virginia, or for that matter, in Bridgeview, Ill.; or Jersey City, N.J.; or Dearborn, Mich., where residents are routinely subjected to rallies and marches for Hezbollah and other terror groups, along with calls to pray blasted over mosque loudspeakers five times a day. These places look and sound more like little Cairos than any American city, and they provide perfect cover for Muslim terrorists and their supporters.[2]

They may not be slaughtering goats in your neighborhood yet, but incursions of Muslim populations bring changes not limited to culture. Sometimes there are attempts to influence local legislation. In the Islamic legal system, the state is an enforcer of religious law. The spread of Islam will necessarily occasion attempts to nudge aside the American system, which enshrines religious freedom.

Though sharia still has a low profile in America, many Muslim communities in Britain have established tribunals that operate in defiance of the legal system that was the incubator of liberty under law. Only a few time zones away from America, a civilizational revo-lution is taking place. Is the threat of sharia in America occasionally overstated? Undoubtedly. But the Muslim revolution in Europe started small as well.

Proponents of sharia are energized by their belief that the state ought to disseminate and enforce the faith—a view that is obviously incompatible with the U.S. Constitution. If the hubbub over sharia seems premature, consider the folly of waiting until it becomes a far more pressing problem, far harder to correct.

Some states have already tried to counteract the imposition of "foreign laws" in judicial rulings, a move obviously (and appropri-ately) aimed at sharia, but federal courts have ruled, absurdly, that it is unconstitutional to single out the source of the threat by name. So we are left to pass laws suggesting that we need just as much protec-tion from Scandinavian or Asian jurisprudence. Whatever. If we must jump through semantic hoops, it is well worth it to make clear that while we are the most welcoming nation in human history, we will not be hospitable to attempts to subvert our system of laws.

Our only options in Iran are appeasement and war.

When the Obama administration foisted on the United States a disastrous nuclear arms deal with the Iranian regime, we were told that there was no reasonable alternative. "The choice we face is ulti-mately between diplomacy and some form of war," the president warned.[3] I suppose *every* choice in international relations is "ulti-mately between diplomacy and some form of war," but Obama meant that war would follow if we renounced *his* brand of soft diplomacy, the variety that has empowered terrorists since he took office.

With his rhetorical question, "How can we in good conscience justify war before we've tested a diplomatic agreement that achieves our objectives?" Obama proposed a classic false choice. There is another kind of diplomacy, the kind that makes clear we will not be trifled with, misbehavior will not be rewarded, and relations will not be normalized until there is evidence of compliance with acceptable behavior.

We used to take such stances. When Iraq invaded Kuwait in 1990, though war was an obvious option, we tried diplomacy first— but not the appeasing kind that would have rewarded Saddam Hussein for his adventurism. As tensions mounted in the early days of 1991, Secretary of State James Baker traveled to Geneva for talks with Iraq's foreign minister, Tariq Aziz, offering a diplomatic resolution with one unshakeable condition: Iraq must withdraw from Kuwait immediately. The Iraqis failed to comply, and the resulting brief war brought about the only acceptable result.

This does not mean that diplomatic loggerheads always lead to war. Tough American diplomatic stances have restrained global mischief since we rose to superpower status. In history's highest-stakes example, an American nuclear arsenal, backed by consistent opposition to communism, made certain that the Cold War did not turn hot. Ronald Reagan's refusal to budge on the "Star Wars" Strategic Defense Initiative brought the Soviet Union to its knees.

Iran presents unique challenges but also a unique opportunity. Many of its younger citizens are fed up with the theocratic reign of oppressive mullahs. A patient regimen of tough sanctions coupled with consistent outreach to pro-democracy Iranians could bring about a revolution that lifts the country out of the dark ages that began with the rise of the Ayatollah Khomeini and the seizure of U.S. hostages in 1979. It was no accident that the hostage crisis ended the day Reagan took office. Iran knew its days of manipulating the feckless Jimmy Carter were over. Khomeini himself recognized that Reagan would not submit to additional months of humiliation.

The Obama presidency has delivered different lessons. As the nuclear deal went into effect in January 2016, a U.S. Navy vessel drifted into Iranian territorial waters. In an atmosphere of mutual respect, a resolution would have been reached within minutes. Instead, the Iranians seized and disarmed ten American sailors, displaying them on their knees with their hands clasped behind their heads. President Obama and Secretary of State Kerry actually expressed *appreciation* for the treatment of our sailors, showing the Iranians and the world that a U.S. administration will tolerate humiliation of our servicemen to pad the narrative that the deal with Iran was a good one. Suffice it to say that America is not at its strongest when anything short of beheading draws expressions of gratitude.

So unless a new administration reverses the current unhealthy course, Iran will continue to enjoy billions of dollars freed for its use while pursuing nuclear armament without sufficient U.S. or international oversight. With Iran's oft-stated goal of the destruction of Israel and its habit of facilitating terror worldwide, it is this perilous course and not a return to realistic sanctions that is a more likely path to war.

There is no military strategy that can defeat terrorists.

Democrats are not the only people who say we can't defeat terrorism militarily. Libertarians and even the occasional pessimistic conservative have been seen wringing their hands and shaking their heads at the suggestion of actually fighting and winning this most confounding of all wars.

It's true that armed obliteration of the enemy is not the only route to success. We must maintain sharp-eyed intelligence to guard against new waves of jihadists, and we must also show that we are willing to rebuild and restore relations with regimes that rehabilitate themselves. But before we embark on some Middle Eastern Marshall Plan, we have to remember what comes first—winning the war.

The war against global jihad won't end as World War II did, with the representatives of vanquished states signing an unconditional surrender. They will have to be suppressed by the military might of an American-led coalition until there remains only an occasional brushfire, followed by continuing vigilance for years to come.

But how do we get there?

When people say there is not a military solution to a war on terror, they usually mean there is no solution they are willing to embrace. We are not a warlike people. We do not look for places to throw around our considerable weight. We are not an imperial tyrant. But when war has been a moral necessity, we have responded with determination and success. War gave birth to this nation. American force ended two world wars, has restrained much evil in the Middle East, and could succeed yet again if we found the will to prevail.

That is an admittedly hard road. It would exact a heavy toll not only on our terrorist enemies but on countless non-combatants. No war has been won without collateral damage. But the cost of additional decades of an insufficient response to global jihad would be much greater.

So we have choices. We can continue to shuffle our feet amid talk of "containing" ISIS and its fellow jihadists, or we can recover our war footing and do something about it. A new president committed to rebuilding our military can call on a fighting force that would respond without hesitation if it were finally given a path to victory. Years of looking for an exit strategy have led us to an unsatisfactory place. It is time to start looking for a *success* strategy, preparing for the unavoidable costs in blood and treasure. The alternatives are simply unacceptable.

Throughout history, there has been only one formula for victory: kill enough of the enemy to make him stop fighting. This is how we won the Revolutionary War, World Wars I and II, and the Gulf War. Our failure to meet that requirement is why we lost in Vietnam.

This is not a conventional conflict with an identifiable nation-state, fought according to the recognized rules of warfare. We face an enemy sprawled across several nations, crouching in caves, lurking in urban alleys and on rooftops, pouring out across deserts and over mountains. But we can find them, and we can kill them.

It will be hard enough to watch, even without the detractors who will say we are the monsters for actually trying to win. The Bush administration deserves credit for taking the war to the parts of the world filled with those who wish to kill us, but it failed to kill enough of the enemy to achieve victory.

Some friends of mine who saw multiple tours in Iraq and Afghanistan are fond of saying we built too many schools and water treatment plants and didn't blow up enough terrorists. But there is a time and place for both, in the proper order. Once we have defeated enough jihadists to compel their rehabilitation, we can be a magnanimous victor. On that magnificent day, our heroes in uniform, appreciative that they were at last unshackled and empowered to win, will tell us it was worth it.

The Guantanamo Bay detention facility should be closed.

I have been fortunate enough to walk among some of the forgotten heroes of our war effort: the men and women meeting the challenge of terror in our own hemisphere, on an island enclave a short boat ride from our shores.

The year 2006 was not a good one for our war effort. Americans were developing a weariness that would contribute to the election of Barack Obama, images of the Abu Ghraib prison abuses were still fresh, and anti-war politicians were growing bolder in their assertions that our war effort was not just ill-fated but ignoble. That year I visited Guantanamo with a group of writers and broadcasters.

What exactly are we supposed to do with combatants plucked from the field of battle? They are not entitled to prosecution in our criminal courts with the due process rights of American citizens. Nor are they subject to the Geneva Conventions, which protect the uniformed soldiers of a belligerent state that itself "accepts and applies" the conventions. They are not prisoners, since they have not been convicted of anything. Gitmo is not a jail filled with inner-city gang members. It is a camp filled with detainees removed, fortunately, from the battlefield. Many have been released over the years, only to return to that battlefield and fight us again.

Barack Obama, insisting that Guantanamo is not useful, has promised to close it. In fact, he says, it actually hurts the war effort. Not useful? It keeps at least a few terrorists from killing us. I can imagine no higher use. As for the tired old line that Guantanamo is a "recruiting tool" for terrorists, the problem is that our mere *existence* is a recruiting tool. Does the president believe that if we just let the detainees go or relocate them to the United States then jihadist bloodlust will abate? Please.

Why would anyone seek to move these terrorists to U.S. soil? Maybe it's the hope that their prosecution in American courtrooms would put the American war effort itself on trial, delivering the comeuppance that war critics have long believed this country deserves.

The U.S. forces at Guantanamo deserve our eternal gratitude for their labors in that lonely outpost, matching wits every day with detainees who would kill them where they stand. The sense of duty and honor among those troops is inspiring. A visit to Guantanamo reveals an array of amenities afforded to savage killers who have never before enjoyed such cleanliness, abundant and good food, and medical care (better than that available to many Americans). And the federal government is more accommodating to the terrorists' religious sensibilities than to those of the Little Sisters of the Poor. White-gloved young Americans deliver Korans, and floors are painted with arrows pointing to Mecca so the detainees know which way to turn for their prayers.

In return, our service men and women are treated to death threats, verbal abuse, and the promise of revenge should any of their charges slip free. Velcro patches obscure the names on their uniforms lest their identities be divulged to outsiders, wittingly or unwittingly, by a visiting attorney. Guards are not permitted to examine outgoing pouches. Families could be a Google search away from a terrorist bounty.

Obama's charge that the detention of captured jihadists at Guantanamo is "contrary to our values" indicates how badly he misunderstands those values. Detention facilities for enemy combatants must not be closed until the war effort is over. The president may reduce the number of men held there, but the advances of ISIS make it hard for him to abandon it altogether. There is no way to know when Guantanamo will no longer be of value, but one thing is certain: moving its detainees to American soil is a completely unacceptable option.

The Middle East is not ready for democracy.

Nations with violent jihadists among their population are not usually burning with a desire for Western-style political institutions. But is there something in the DNA of such cultures that renders them wholly unreceptive to the political ideas of the Enlightenment?

"Those people have been at war with each other for centuries," say the self-described "realists." "Let's just let 'em kill each other and sort it out afterward." The first statement is true, but we have to ask, Will it be that way forever? Are we so convinced of the irreconcilability of Muslim nations that we have to throw up our hands and prepare for perpetual war? As for the perhaps appealing prospect of letting the terrorist factions "kill each other," the problem is that they like to kill other people too—for example, Christians and Jews in America, Israel, and elsewhere.

It is as if we were waiting for nations steeped in ancient hatreds to shake off the cobwebs of the past before holding them to higher standards. This is classic cart-before-the-horse. First we have to show the world that those who wish to kill us will be killed first. Then we show the world that we will reach out to friends and former enemies as partners in trade and encouragers of liberty. There is not an oppressed nation on earth that does not contain huddled masses yearning to breathe free in their own lands. They are not always in the majority; sometimes the expression of such passions can get them jailed, tortured, or killed.

It is human nature to cling to what we know, even if it is not good for us. A quarter-century after the fall of the Soviet Union, nostalgia for the safety nets of communism occasionally arises in its former subjects. Freedom is scary. The suffocating womb of totalitarianism is still a womb, and not everyone wants to come out. Reform in the Middle East will face the same resistance. But we are not trying to turn Iraq into Indiana. No one seeks to erect overnight a full-blown Jeffersonian democracy in the Islamic world, where the chief obstacle to such a project might be the religion itself. But while there are no guarantees of success in spreading stability across the Middle East, there are dark consequences for not trying.

Small victories for the Islamic reformers could start the ball rolling. You don't have to be a pedal-to-the-metal "nation-builder" to believe that freedom is a human instinct, even if it has usually been stifled throughout history.

13

MARRIAGE

States have no right to define marriage.

When an activist Supreme Court forced gay marriage on the states in June 2015, supporters of traditional marriage understandably lamented for faith-based and ideological reasons. But complaints against a court ruling must have a constitutional basis; we should not look to courts to satisfy our individual political or religious tastes. The court's gay marriage ruling in *Obergefell v. Hodges* was wrong not because I am a conservative and a Christian, but because it strayed so promiscuously from the Constitution.

If the Constitution permits, requires, or forbids something, it usually says so. This is not to say there are no grey areas, but gay marriage is simply not one of them. And in writing for the majority, Justice Anthony Kennedy did us the favor of revealing the basis of his argument, which has nothing to do with the law and everything to do with his feelings. "No longer may this liberty be denied," he declared, with no reference to any constitutional text. "No union is more profound than marriage, for it embodies the highest ideals of love, fidelity, devotion, sacrifice and family. In forming a marital union, two people become something greater than once they were." No kidding. And nicely said. But a Supreme Court opinion should not read like a Hallmark card.

Identifying marriage as a "keystone of our social order," (right again), Kennedy noted that the plaintiffs sought "equal dignity in the eyes of the law." That they did. If only someone on the winning side could tell us why the desire for "equal dignity," a concept not mentioned in the Constitution, entitles someone to a victory at the Supreme Court.

It's a fair bet that none of the Founding Fathers ever gave a thought to same-sex marriage. But in their wisdom, they gave us the Ninth and Tenth Amendments to the Constitution, which might have been titled "What to Do When Something Comes Up that We Didn't Think About."

The Tenth Amendment is the linchpin of states' rights, a key concept in our federal system. From its birth, the United States of America was a confederation of states, with no pretense of legal uniformity throughout the union. Life in Pennsylvania was not going to be the same as life in Georgia. Accordingly, the Tenth Amendment affirms that matters unaddressed in the Constitution are left to the states: "The powers not delegated to the United States by the Constitution, nor prohibited by it to the States, are reserved to the States respectively, or to the people."

The Ninth Amendment—"The enumeration in the Constitution, of certain rights, shall not be construed to deny or disparage others retained by the people"—reinforces the right to local self-government by allowing the citizens of the several states to establish the laws they choose through their own legislative processes.

The law of marriage, therefore, is properly left to the states. Those wishing to recognize same-sex marriage may do so, and states not wishing to don't have to. That, by the way, is how abortion will be handled after *Roe v. Wade* is overturned. This is what America looks like when it is governed according to the Constitution.

Gay marriage has no effect on society at large.

"What difference does it make to your marriage if gays are allowed to marry?" Anyone arguing for unique legal recognition of man-woman marriage had better be ready for this one.

It's a fair question, and personal distaste is not a sufficient answer. Proponents of gay marriage have successfully appealed to the American instinct to live and let live, which would be enough if gay unions happened in a vacuum. But they do not. So what are the objective arguments against same-sex marriage? I'm not asking about the pluses and minuses of gay marriage itself. Gays may marry any time they wish, anywhere they wish, as an exercise of individual liberty and religious freedom. The public policy debate is over the legal recognition of such marriages. As soon as such recognition is made compulsory, it becomes everybody's business. So what are the principled reasons to oppose gay marriage?

What a society allows and disallows is a window to its belief system. Recognition of the sexual differences established by God is under attack. The establishment of gay marriage is an assertion that sex does not matter as long as there is love and commitment. People are free to believe that, of course, but they are also free to differ.

The complementarity of male and female has made marriage—always and everywhere—the starting point for families and thus for the continuation of the species. Since same-sex couples cannot fill that role, treating their unions as marriages of equal status fundamentally changes the meaning of the institution. Again, people are free to cast this aside and reshape marriage to suit their wishes, but those cleaving to its original intent have eons of history to rely on.

Dismissing the importance of sexual complementarity in marriage leads straight to the question of adoption by same-sex couples. There are now many gay adoptive parents raising kids in loving households. But are we to cast aside the preference for giving children both a mother and father? Motherhood and fatherhood are not identical, and neither role is dismissible. Children ought to enjoy the nurture and guidance that a man and woman provide cooperatively. With each passing generation, more kids are raised without the benefit of both a mother and father, but that does not invalidate the value of the ideal.

Many adoption agencies are faith-based. Are we to tell them that they are forbidden from seeking to place children preferentially with a married man and woman?

Gays seeking to marry are not necessarily soldiers in the gender-obliteration movement, but the vital differences between men and women are why the normalization of gay marriage is a radical prospect that people have every right to argue against without a shred of homophobia.

The gay marriage trend is irreversible.

It is easy to throw up our hands and say all the horses are out of the barn. Will we ever reinstill the importance of abstinence until marriage? Can couples rediscover the gravity of marriage vows? Will men reacquaint themselves with the obligation to stay in families that they start?

Sometimes trends are linear, but sometimes pendulums swing back. In the years following *Roe v. Wade,* America was coldly cavalier about the life of the unborn. Decades of work by the pro-life movement has moved public opinion into a renewed hesitancy to cast aside life in the womb, especially late in the pregnancy. Pro-life convictions are not unanimous, but in the tug-of-war of public opinion, the rope has been pulled toward a broader acceptance of abortion restrictions and a broader distaste for late-term abortion.

Not long after Colorado legalized marijuana, a poll revealed about half of the state's voters regretted the move.[1] A friend of mine who lives in Boulder was on the fence about it when the measure passed. Now he sees the disadvantages: "It's getting a lot harder to find somebody to patch a roof early in the morning."

Anecdotes aren't necessarily evidence of a full-scale public change of heart. But they show that minds can be changed. It doesn't always work, but when the stakes are high and the case can be made, it is worth the try.

So can the gay marriage juggernaut be slowed? The odds are stacked against the effort, with public opinion growing more tolerant of gay marriage year after year. Throw in the full weight of popular culture and the widely-leveled slander that only hate can motivate any opposition, and the mountain looks very high.

But the goal need not be a return to a time when same-sex unions were scarcely discussed. It would be a major victory to reach an equilibrium in which adherents and opponents could hold their views without fear of suppression. From adoption agencies wishing to place children with married heterosexual couples to bakeries wishing to stay out of the gay wedding business, there are stances widely maligned as bigotry which are nothing of the kind. When such beliefs are afforded protection (and when the Supreme Court corrects its *Obergefell* error), we can create a level playing field of discussion over whether gay marriage equality is to be enacted state by state.

Opposing same-sex marriage is like opposing mixed-race marriage.

This misconception is the result of one of the central claims of the gay-rights movement: that being gay is kind of like being black—it's an immutable characteristic, like race.

The problem with this claim is that while racial differences are wholly irrelevant to the human condition, sexual differences are central to it. Marrying someone of another race does not affect the purpose of marriage. Marrying someone of the same sex is a wholesale reboot of the marriage concept.

Interracial marriage has been practiced from time immemorial, while same-sex marriage has been a topic of conversation, historically speaking, for about five minutes. There is no basis in the history of moral philosophy for objection to interracial marriage; objection to homosexuality has been a virtually universal moral norm since men and women—and marriage—were created.

One can argue that sometimes enlightenment has been slow to arrive. After all, how long have women had the vote? But the social equality of women is self-evident. There is nothing about being female that warrants exclusion from the political process. But the only argument that can be made for same-sex marriage is that some people want it.

Gay-marriage proponents are free to seek their chosen revisions wherever and whenever they like. Suggesting they are standing on the shoulders of those who have fought for racial equality is an insult to those crusaders—and to logic.

Monogamy is obsolete.

As soon as monogamy settled in as a societal ideal, someone probably objected—I'm guessing it was a man—that it was somehow against human nature. This is actually quite correct. Sexual attraction is a powerful instinct. Monogamy's civilizing effect is to restrain us from acting on that attraction indiscriminately. But yes, much of humanity, left to its own unfettered intents, would pursue mate after mate after mate.

Morality involves the willful suppression of our basest instincts—to lie, to cheat, to steal, and so forth. We generally do not hear that we should loosen up on theft because of our larcenous nature. But we do get an occasional earful that the whole monogamy thing is a relic best shelved. Not in favor of polygamy (except in some corners), but in favor of relaxing those old confining rules that say we are to save ourselves sexually for marriage and then remain married to one person for life.

The notion of one sexual partner for life has become a marginalized anachronism. How many people can claim to adhere to that standard? Evaluating a potential spouse, we're now taught, should include a test drive. If the spin around the block is less than satisfactory, better to discard your would-be soulmate before making the big down payment.

Once married, husbands and wives concoct endless justifications for straying outside the marital bond. "He doesn't excite me." "She doesn't get me." "My needs aren't being met." Then they embark on an exhausting path of deception and betrayal, expending far more energy than would have been required to repair their marriages.

Sometimes there is no deception, as when couples decide to pursue the depravity of the "open relationship," freeing both to indulge the low instinct of giving in to that "human nature" of seeking sexual variety. There may not be deception, but there is still betrayal. Both spouses will have betrayed the institution of marriage, intentionally shutting the door on the possibility of growth and commitment that only an exclusive commitment can provide.

The behavioral decay of the 1960s set the stage for decades of redefinition of what was acceptable. By 1990, University of Colorado football coach Bill McCartney had seen about enough and gathered a nucleus of men for the purpose of committing themselves and others to biblical principles in their marriages and other relationships. A quarter-century later, Promise Keepers still exists. I remember the October 1997 rally on the National Mall in Washington, D.C., featuring hundreds of thousands of participants. It seemed at the time as though a continuing slide in godly behavior was being met with pockets of resistance that continue today.

We can follow our urges, which lead to ruined marriages, shattered trust, and scattered children. Or we can try to do better.

Kids are resilient; divorce is no big deal.

We've all heard of husbands and wives who cast their marriages against the rocks, rationalizing that it's better to tear apart their children's homes when they are younger. "They're resilient when they're young," the excuse goes. "They'll get over it."

How nice for parents to cut and run because they didn't get exactly what they bargained for. What a delicious power, to be able to hit a big reset button on a whim and cast the children into a nightmare of two homes, maybe in distant cities, two bedrooms, two Christmases, two dramas of single parenthood, and then, hey, maybe a new person in Mommy or Daddy's bed?

This heart-rending scene hardly raises an eyebrow any more. And the fact is that kids are indeed resilient. In a world of undercommitted men and women, they had better be.

Of course there are marriages that need to end. In cases of unredeemable abuse or irreparably shattered trust, the victim is justified in packing up the kids and venturing out in search of peace and stability. But that's not why most marriages end today.

Most marriages end today because of laziness. Those vows are hard, and keeping them takes work. So many people are so focused on a daily barometer of happiness that they lose sight of the source of real joy: committing to God, to our spouses, and to our children for the duration. If we strive to be the best husbands and wives and parents we can be, we won't have as much time to wallow in our own petty complaints. Meanwhile, the families we create will radiate the gratitude that brings us the greatest chances for real happiness.

It doesn't always work out that way, of course. But every time a mom or dad decides to pack it in, a promise made to the kids is destroyed. Every child has the right to expect an intact family throughout childhood. If the parents have to make some sacrifices, that's part of the bargain.

How many parents who have abandoned their kids resort to the classic rationalization "Better for them to have two peaceful households than one in conflict"? Here's an idea: resolve the conflict. Get your act together and keep the promises you made on your wedding day and on the day those children were born.

Divorces will happen, and sometimes they are justified. But no one should minimize the atom bomb dropped on children when Mom and Dad don't want to keep their promises any more.

I watched a documentary a few years ago about the life and work of the underappreciated Beatle George Harrison, a cultural figure of great import but maybe not the most loyal and devoted husband. Nevertheless, he and his second wife, Olivia, remained married for more than thirty years, until his death in 2001. Her advice for achieving a long marriage is brilliant in its simplicity: "Don't get divorced."

Take the commitment not to divorce, add the energy and love that can result in actual joy, and miracles can happen. Children cannot always say so, but even in a marriage's rough patches, they would far rather see Mom and Dad work through it than just chuck it all and make them cope.

14

ELECTIONS

There is too much money in politics.

Here's an old reliable you hear from people all along the political spectrum. "Tell you what's wrong with politics," says the conservative trucker or liberal actor, "too much money."

Not true. What exactly is "too much money"? Every political contribution represents a decision to support a certain candidate or cause. Who is to say when that support reaches a point of excess?

Political dollars can be misspent, as when they finance the degrading noise of bitter ad campaigns or influence the behavior of officials. But if an official changes a vote because of a big check, that's not the money's fault, it's the official's fault. The National Rifle Association contributes to conservatives not to *turn* them pro-gun, but because they already *are* pro-gun. Labor unions aren't looking to liberalize candidates ambivalent about unions. They are looking to reward those who are already sympathetic.

Citizens' discontent with the millions spent on ad campaigns is often just misplaced aggression. Seeing enormous amounts spent so that Candidate A can bludgeon Candidate B on TV, we think that the money could be better spent. It surely could, but we should always restrain ourselves when seeking to make decisions about how other people spend their money.

Campaign spending is speech. As such, it should not be restricted. I confess to a quirky dream of removing all limits from political contributions, coupled with instant online disclosure of where the money came from. Citizens could celebrate or condemn every new revelation of who got how much from whom. The mega-rich would be free to prop up whomever they please, of course, but last time I checked, America was filled with wealthy conservatives and wealthy liberals. Completely free political spending, therefore, would not tilt the playing field. And we commoners would be free to judge campaigns based on the checks they cashed.

The freedom to contribute politically is such an irritant to some that proposals for publicly funded campaigns keep cropping up. This hideous idea would hijack private spending and dump it into another government program. Only slightly less absurd are the fraudulently titled "clean election initiatives," which subsidize campaigns and candidates as a reward for jumping through various hoops. Even if America were not drowning in debt, public funding of campaigns would be an affront to taxpayers, who deserve to be able to contribute to whomever they please.

Many of the complaints about money in politics come from struggling campaigns that are being outspent. Campaign coffers are an applause meter. If a candidate is racking up big contributions, maybe it's because a lot of people support that candidate. If another candidate's fundraising draws crickets and tumbleweeds, that may reveal the opposite.

Running for office is expensive and always will be. Complaints miss the point. Political donors are doing what they have a right to do.

Voter ID is voter suppression.

Conservatives are used to accusations of racism, misogyny, environmental depredation, and various other forms of cruelty and wickedness. But the accusation that stands out for particular absurdity is that strong voter identification laws are intended to suppress votes.

As the official spokesman for Everybody Fighting for Voter ID, I authorize the following proclamation: We favor voting by all voters who can meet the simple standard of proving they are who they say they are when they show up at a polling place. Nevertheless, because voter ID imposes a burden no heavier than that required to drive a car or board an airplane, we are told we do not want minorities or the elderly or some other demographic group to vote. This charge, aside from being false, insults the very people opponents supposedly champion.

Acquiring an ID is one of the easiest things a human being can do. Non-drivers may get an official photo ID at most driver's license offices. Various states accept a wide range of other identification, from passports to property tax bills. Securing an ID entails such trivial cost and effort that it is hard to imagine a functional citizen's being deterred. The suggestion that blacks or Hispanics are somehow unable to complete this task is quite a putdown.

One can argue that the elderly or disabled may face challenges, but they are already familiar with the obstacles of life, meeting most of them with grace and determination every day. If voting is important, anyone in any condition will do what is necessary to get an ID to perform that task.

The prevalence of voter fraud is the subject of debate. Opponents of voter ID suggest it is virtually nonexistent, while supporters sometimes assert that it is rampant. It surely exists to some degree, probably more than we know, and that's where the case is made. Is the integrity of elections important? Yes. Are there simple things we can do to make election fraud more difficult? Yes. Are there any disadvantages to taking these steps? No. End of argument.

The howling of liberals at voter ID proposals suggests that reducing voter fraud is not a priority for them. Now why might that be?

We should ditch the Electoral College.

I was actually inclined to agree with this one well into adulthood. As I charted a course through talk shows in various cities, chronicling a presidential election every four years, it took decades for me to appreciate the system the Constitution establishes for electing our chief executive.

It was not the razor-thin election of 2000 that changed my mind. The popular-vote margin that year went to Al Gore by about one-half of a percentage point, or a half-million votes out of over 100 million cast, while the 271-266 margin in the Electoral College made George W. Bush president, to my obvious relief. But I had come off the fence about our presidential election process four years earlier at the Democratic national convention in Chicago, oddly enough, as I watched Bill Clinton nominated for a second term.

A dirty little secret of conservative commentators is that we have more fun at Democratic conventions than at our own. There's no better place to escape the soundtrack of our daily lives and enjoy stimulating political conversation with Americans of wildly differing views. In the midst of one such conversation, someone trotted out the old saw that presidential elections should be one person–one vote "because that's what the nation was founded on and that's what democracy is all about." Another interlocutor, a professor, offered an insightful double correction: If it's contrary to the Constitution, it is obviously *not* what the nation was founded on, and while one vote per person is emblematic of direct democracy, the Founders intentionally shunned that method of selecting a president.

That Democrat professor helped me realize that the Framers of the Constitution intended only one part of the federal government to be chosen by direct popular vote—the House of Representatives, whose large size and frequency of election make it closest to the people. U.S. senators were to be chosen by state legislatures, as they were until 1913, when the Sixteenth Amendment changed the system to direct popular vote.

As pressure mounts to dismantle the Electoral College, every citizen should take to heart what the president is supposed to be. He or she is not our individual national representative, like some super-congressman, but the chief executive of the union of states. The citizens of each state get a vote in the awarding of their state's electors. So yes, a voter in Laramie, Wyoming, may have a smidgen more per-capita voting clout than a voter in Los Angeles. But so what? Wyoming has three electors, California fifty-five. The L.A. voters are casting ballots for a far larger prize. Liberals like the idea of presidential elections by popular vote because populous cities lean left in their voting habits.

It's fair to ask if conservatives like the Electoral College because it increases the influence of less populous states, which tend to be more conservative. They probably do. But someday a Democrat will lose the popular vote but win the majority of electors, and I will still want the original system maintained.

Everybody hates negative advertising.

We often hear that voters want candidates to stop attacking their rivals and focus on the issues. But the fact is that negative ads often work, which is why candidates keep running them. Even people who complain about them soak up their messages like sponges. Which do you think raises more eyebrows in the closing days of a tight election, a candidate's hundredth commercial featuring a policy statement or a new blast identifying his opponent as a scoundrel?

While people don't like negative ads about candidates they support, they are far more tolerant of negative ads about candidates they oppose. Such ads actually serve multiple purposes. They provide talking points for arguments against rivals, and they can reveal the focus and strategy of the camp running the ad. The U.S. senators in the 2016 GOP presidential field touted their lawmaking experience. The governors in the field brushed that aside, pointing to their executive experience running a state. The political outsiders proclaimed a pox on both houses, offering options for voters seeking candidates who had never even run for office.

When we say we don't like negative advertising, we're often trying to sound high-minded, as when people said they weren't glued to the O. J. Simpson trial. It's human nature to be drawn to a public fight, largely because most of us lead comparatively mannerly lives. We don't spend much of the day locked in adversarial struggles (one hopes), so TV ad wars can be a lowbrow escape.

But not all negative advertising debases our cultural discourse. It often points out some flaw in an opponent—a troubling statement, an errant vote—which is fair game. The annoying negative ads are the ones that stoop to juvenile insults. Sadly, these probably work, too. And the temptation to respond in kind, for fear of seeming complacent or unwilling to "fight back," can be powerful.

Political ad wars take place in a heated arena where the combatants know they have our attention in thirty- and sixty-second bursts. The public's famously shortening attention span encourages campaigns to generate more heat than light. But in principle, there is nothing unethical about negative advertising if it is not misleading. Any candidate seeking an office has two jobs, after all: to explain why he is a wonderful choice, and to explain why his rivals are not.

The "establishment" forces moderate candidates on us.

The complaints are loud and long, and I have sometimes joined in the chorus. I have often felt frustrated in my search for a consistent conservative candidate in the mold of Ronald Reagan by honorable but underwhelming nominees. The drill became familiar on the talk shows I hosted in the run-ups to 2008 and 2012: steadfast conservatives would yearn for voters to coalesce behind their chosen candidates then watch with slumped shoulders as John McCain and Mitt Romney delivered their convention acceptance speeches.

As the years have passed, it has become the conventional wisdom that these candidates were foisted on an unwilling Republican electorate by the "Establishment." This perception shaped the 2016 presidential primary contests.

But I have found myself on a quest: to make sure that if Republicans are displeased with a given year's standard-bearer, they have no one to blame but themselves. No one made state after state elevate McCain or Romney; voters did so of their own free will. No puppet masters manipulated Republicans in the privacy of the voting booths. McCain and Romney won fair and square. I have tried to help frustrated conservatives realize two things: voters were not as far right as they might have liked in those elections, and if the party wants a solidly conservative nominee, it requires two things: an effective salesman of conservatism and a voting public willing to listen. The 2016 campaign began as a grand experiment to see if those two things could actually happen. Ted Cruz came admirably close and might well have been the nominee in a field that did not contain Donald Trump.

Nevertheless, there *is* an establishment. It was entertaining to listen to the kingmakers (as Phyllis Schlafly dubbed them long ago in *A Choice Not an Echo*) deny their own existence in 2016, insisting that the term has no meaning, and that there is no cabal waiting to throw obstacles in the path of muscular conservatism.

Right.

The establishment is made up of the donor class, the consultant class, many in the pundit class, and a large portion of the elected Republican officials who talked a strong game on the campaign trail but withered under the pressures of actual governing. It is apparently very hard to keep promises when faced with disdain from the media, the cocktail party circuit, and Democrats naturally full of themselves after decades of success.

The establishment surely exists. It spends money and exerts power to soften the sharp edges of bold conservatism. But in any election year, voters hold the ultimate power. If enough of them are willing to push back against the middling tastes of the power brokers, anything can happen, as the primary election season of 2016 revealed.

15

THE ECONOMY

Income inequality is a problem.

Consider the meaning of the term "income inequality": some incomes are high and some are low. When has it ever been otherwise in world history?

"Inequality" is bad only when there ought to be equality. Inequality based on race or creed, for example, is intolerable. But *income*? Where did we get the notion that incomes need to be equalized in defiance of the free marketplace?

To be fair, income-equality turf-pounders are not (yet) trying to literally *equalize* what we all make. They are simply complaining that the low end of the income scale is too low and the high end is too high. Their pernicious remedy is to drain the incomes of the upper earners for redistribution to those nearer the bottom.

This is the eternal economic mission of the Left. The difference today is that the slogan "income inequality" suggests that the range of incomes is objectively disordered and requires equalizing.

Let's begin at the low end of incomes. Poverty is a problem, especially if you are living in it. The good news is that a free-market economy offers the best hope for climbing out of poverty into the middle class and even further upward from there. Not everyone succeeds at this, but opportunities abound in a capitalist economy. The tragic truth is that a high percentage of Americans in poverty are there not because of a flaw in the economic system but because of a catastrophe of some sort or, more frequently, a track record of poverty-perpetuating bad decisions.

In the last few years, leaders and experts across the political spectrum, from the conservative former senator and presidential candidate Rick Santorum to the scholars at the liberal Brookings Institution, have pointed out that if you do three simple things—get a high school diploma, wait till you're twenty-one to get married and have children (in that order), and get a full-time job—you have a 98 percent chance of avoiding poverty. So much for the nonsense about the American economic deck being stacked against the people.

And while we're exploding myths, let's dispense with the vacuous notion that one person's wealth necessarily comes at the expense of another person. In fact, the opposite is true. Who are the job creators, after all?

If left unmolested by punitive taxation, the wealthy will create jobs, pay better, and give more to charity. But this truth is obscured by the claim that wealth is a zero-sum game—that the gains of one portion of the economy must be offset by the losses of another.

Every quintile of the income chart has shown improvement since 1995. It is a fraudulent model that pie slices can only grow by diminishing other slices. In a free-market economy, the entire pie gets bigger.

Even if redistributionists' economic fantasies were true, their favored prescription—soaking high-income Americans with even more taxes—would fail. We don't have enough rich people to bleed dry for the sake of the masses below, and even if we did, such piracy would suppress investment, which creates jobs, which help people improve their lot in life.

Respect economic liberty. Let people keep more of their money. Encourage wise decisions in early adulthood. Follow those rules, and more people will move toward wealth. That's how the well-off did well in the first place. The politics of envy helps no one but its preachers.

The middle class is disappearing.

A corollary of the income-inequality scare tactic is the notion that the middle class is vanishing. The popular image is of a predatory upper class victimizing folks in the middle and forcing them down into poverty. The middle class is indeed smaller than in past decades, but the income-inequality warriors don't want you to know one of the main reasons why: many in the middle class are moving on up.

Examining Americans' five income tiers, Pew Research found that the middle class shrank from 61 percent of households in 1971 to 50 percent of households in 2015. But while the combined low and lower-middle tiers grew from 25 percent of households to 29 percent in that period, the combined upper-middle and highest tiers grew by half, from 14 percent of households to 21 percent.[1]

The researchers gave their report an odd subtitle: "The American middle class is losing ground." Did they read their own numbers? In a story about this report, CNN's Tami Luhby joined those prematurely eulogizing the middle class: "The once strong middle class no longer dominates America.... For decades, the middle class had been the core of the country. A healthy middle class kept America strong, experts and politicians said. But more recently, these residents have struggled under stagnating wages and soaring costs. Presidential candidates on both sides of the political aisle are campaigning on ways to bolster the nation's middle class and increase opportunities to climb the economic ladder."[2]

Actually, plenty of people are finding ways to climb the economic ladder. The lower levels are growing a little, but just as higher wage earners are on the move because of choices they made, so too might some income losses be the consequence of less prudent behavior.

The middle class will always be the largest segment of American wage distribution. The best way to help people move out of the lower brackets and into the middle is to support the free markets that create jobs. Happily, this is also the mechanism that will continue to propel middle-class families into the upper ranges.

The rich do not pay enough taxes.

The next time someone suggests that "the rich do not pay their fair share" of taxes, ask what the definition of "fair" is. The answer may be vague. Fairness is a fluid and subjective concept that may differ from person to person or from day to day. Usually the folks suggesting that the wealthy get a free ride on taxes have no idea what they pay; they just know that "they could afford it" if we chose to dig even more deeply into their pockets.

Well, of course they could "afford" it. Someone making a million dollars a year can "afford" to surrender nine hundred thousand dollars of it and still be better off than the vast majority of Americans. Shockingly, there are people—and even politicians—who think that might be a good idea. Before the Reagan presidency, the highest federal marginal income tax rates were at 70 percent. Cutting that by more than half set off an economic boom that lasted a quarter-century.

Our progressive tax system punishes success. The more we make, the higher our tax rate. This is not just economically unwise, it is immoral. Taxes are necessary, but Washington should demand only what is required to run a lean, limited government.

The top 10 percent of America's wage earners make 45 percent of the nation's total income but pay 68 percent of the nation's tax bill.[3] This is highway robbery, curable by a flat tax that would take, for example, 17 percent no matter what the annual income. From Steve Forbes to the former House majority leader Dick Armey to a smattering of recent presidential candidates, many people have floated flat tax plans that are the definition of "fairness." What is fairer than taking 17 percent from the family making fifty thousand dollars and 17 percent from the family making fifty million?

Most flat-tax plans exempt the first forty thousand dollars or so—more for larger families. This makes it easier to sell, but if we are dealing in hard truths, every wage-earner needs to have a stake in U.S. tax policy. If a kid makes ten thousand dollars flipping burgers, he should send in $1,700. A candidate testing that out on the campaign trail will soon have his days free. But it is unhealthy for half of America to have no skin in the tax game; that's what we have now.

A national sales tax is another favorite among reformers. The notion of paying taxes based on what we buy is attractive, and it would be preferable to our current monster of a tax code. But it seems regressive, actually giving top wage-earners a lower tax rate. Do people making two million dollars a year really buy forty times more stuff than people making fifty grand?

Whatever tax reform ideas catch on, we need to end the system that penalizes success. Do not let anyone suggest that the wealthy are enjoying a free ride. The bottom 50 percent of all wage earners make only 12 percent of all income, but their combined tax burden of 3 percent shows that we insulate millions from paying any taxes at all. There are few drugs as addicting as the redistributed wealth of others. Until that habit is kicked, real reform may be nearly impossible.

Government should help create jobs.

This one might raise an eyebrow. Aren't our leaders supposed to create jobs? Don't our politicians crow about the jobs they create? Sure they do. But if job numbers do well during a certain presidency or a certain Congress, no one in government deserves the credit. Our free-market economy is what creates jobs; the best thing government can do is get out of the way and let it happen.

Job creation is one of the best things that can happen in an economy, so elected officials and candidates talk about it a lot. But there is a natural inclination for politicians to frame all issues in terms of what *they* did to improve it. They're not inclined to proclaim that things have improved because they had the wisdom to keep their hands off.

Consider, for example, the constant discussion of government "jobs programs." Your state has jobs programs. Washington promotes jobs programs. Who can't love jobs programs? The problem is that almost all of those jobs programs require government to spend money we don't have and to stick its nose into a marketplace best left alone. Jobs are created when the market needs something to be done. When workers fill those jobs, the process is complete, without any need for government to butt in.

We have been softened up for government intrusion in the job market by tales of President Franklin Roosevelt's New Deal. Sucker-punched by the Depression, Americans were told their only hope was the massive boondoggles (a term coined at that time) cooked up by FDR and his Brain Trust.

The Works Progress Administration "created" countless jobs for which there was no marketplace justification. The popular culture of the day even called attention to it in songs like "WPA," written by Harlem arranger Jesse Stone and recorded by the Mills Brothers and Louis Armstrong:

> WPA, WPA, sleep while you work, while you rest, while
>   you play;
> Lean on your shovel to pass time away...
> Three little letters that make life okay,
> WPA, WPA...

In the decades since, schools have taught that the WPA and the alphabet soup of other New Deal programs saved the nation. Government jobs programs must be a good idea to protect against any economic hiccup, right?

Well, no. Like anything government does, jobs programs invite waste, fraud, and abuse, often without yielding much benefit. Job searches today are largely conducted online and through existing relationships, staffing agencies, and private-sector job fairs, not through interaction with some taxpayer-funded operation.

At the Cato Institute's downsizinggovernment.org, Chris Edwards and Daniel Murphy offer a useful history of these wasted dollars: "[F]ederal employment and training programs don't fill any critical economic need that private markets don't already fill. Instead, the federal programs provide an opportunity for policymakers to show that they are 'doing something' to help the labor market. To policy-makers, federal job training sounds like something that should boost the economy, but five decades of experience indicate otherwise."[4]

Raising the minimum wage helps people.

The economic foolishness most difficult to eradicate is the kind that sounds great to people who don't pay much attention—a population that grows by the day. While liberal politicians try to raise the minimum wage to curry favor with undermotivated workers and to strengthen government's grip on private business, the public approves of this toxic policy because its analysis often goes about a millimeter deep.

Let's try to be smarter. Government has no place telling businesses what to charge or what to pay people. They will offer what they think a job is worth. If they get applicants, it's enough. If they do not, they need to pay more.

If government forces wages higher, businesses will respond by cutting jobs. Money does not magically appear, allowing them to pay the artificially increased labor costs. Cities crazily adopting so-called "living wages" (which can run more than double the federal $7.25) are already experiencing job losses.[5]

Now to the radical truth: it is not only a bad idea to have a *higher* minimum wage, it is a bad idea to have any minimum wage at all. If an inner-city shopkeeper could throw five or six bucks per hour at a handful of local kids to clean up or help out, that could be the way off the streets for many. No one would be forced to accept work at that wage. The wonder of marketplace relationships is how they reach an equilibrium between what employers are willing to pay and what employees are willing to work for.

Throw off that equilibrium and you hurt the very people the wage warriors say they are trying to help. The fast-food industry has always been a source of first jobs for the young. Those jobs have been reduced over the years by technology, but if restaurants are forced to pay unrealistic wages, they will lunge toward automation. The *Washington Post*, not exactly a libertarian oracle, quoted an industry consultant who envisioned staffing levels cut in half.[6] Some of those job cuts would be the product of tech advances that would happen anyway, but forced wage increases would surely speed the banishment of human workers.

The elimination of the minimum wage would instantly increase youth employment, especially in economically disadvantaged areas. There's nothing more powerful than a rewarded work ethic.

16

THE WORLD

People around the world are fundamentally the same.

If any misconception has blocked the path to clarity about various global concerns, it is the childlike belief that people are basically the same the world over. We share certain biological components and some strands of human nature, but since we are also products of our environment, the widely varying circumstances of life yield an enormous range of outlook and behavior among people who share human DNA but not much else.

In fact, human nature itself accounts for these differences. Man adapts to his conditions, for better or worse. Adaptability may have helped our hunter-gatherer ancestors, but it also causes entire nations to grow comfortable with dictators and theocratic tyrants.

Remember professional oddball Dennis Rodman's bizarre 2014 junket to North Korea, accompanied by some retired NBA players willing to play an exhibition game against the baby-faced monster Kim Jong-Un's national team? Rodman and Kim became buddies of a sort, Kim enjoying a PR bonanza and Rodman drinking from a fresh well of attention. The most memorable images for me—from an accompanying documentary, *Dennis Rodman's Big Bang in Pyong-yang*—were of the adoring, identically dressed crowds gathered not just to watch the game but to express their worshipful zeal for "The Marshal." These people live enslaved and deprived under the despotic rule of a lunatic. And they are thrilled. There are dissidents tucked into this suffering nation somewhere, but good luck finding them. And good luck surviving if you are one of them.

And yet their devotion is real, as was the fidelity of countless millions under Soviet oppression, as is the approval of Cubans who still embrace the Castro regime, even with a free country ninety miles off their shores.

Across the Middle East, the pressure to fall in line with horrific regimes is not just political but religious. The throngs who celebrated 9/11, perverted by years of indoctrination, will celebrate the next attack. Pockets of resistance are found wherever there is oppression, but the lesson of history is that people will follow a variety of directions, for good or evil.

And it can happen quickly. It has often been noted that Germany was "the most civilized nation on earth," yet it fell under Hitler's spell in the blink of an eye. Islamist revolutionary leaders have convinced millions in just the last few decades that the Western world is the Great Satan.

In America, a land blessed with freedom, the rose-colored glasses business is booming. How willingly we ignore the realities of a world filled with poisonous cultures sharing few of our concepts of basic rights and decency. This myopia leads us to think that we can bargain with our enemies as we would with our next-door neighbor, that we can find common ground with anyone from ISIS to North Korea. We should always try to maintain peace by identifying shared interests; one hopes, for example, that our commercial relations with China will lure it out of its Marxist cave. But this is not always possible. Sometimes evil must be defeated in war. The human thirst for power and wealth will always spawn tyrants to threaten our freedom and self-determination.

We tend to think that self-government and liberty are the default setting for the human race, that everyone will in time naturally come over to our way of doing things. This is dangerously naïve. Most human beings have lived under dictators and tyrants. If the trend of history is toward liberty, it's a very slow trend. In the meantime, our survival depends on a clear-eyed assessment of the world around us.

Paul Harvey was fond of reminding his listeners, "It is not one world." That doesn't mean we can't make the world better. We really are the shining city on a hill. We just need to know that most of the world lives differently and isn't all that interested in emulating us. That doesn't mean we stop trying.

America should strive to be liked.

It is good for an individual to be liked, but to be dominated by the need for approval is disastrous. A person should be kind and generous, but also wise and vigilant, ready to defend his interests even if it means ruffling feathers. The same is true for our country. We are the most giving and welcoming nation in the history of the world, but we have enemies who will harm us if we let them.

America loves peace, but peace is the fruit of victory. If peace were simply the absence of fighting, unilateral disarmament might bring it about. But it would last only as long as it took for our enemies to realize they could now advance without interruption.

This is why, as scary as the Cold War was, the doctrine of mutual assured destruction was useful in confronting a nuclear-equipped foe. As long as the Soviet Union knew we were not backing down, it was kept at bay. If America had dismantled its nuclear arsenal to show how much we wanted peace, history would have taken a different, and darker, turn.

Ronald Reagan could have given up on a strategic nuclear defense system in 1986 to appease Mikhail Gorbachev. We could have looked the other way when Saddam Hussein invaded Kuwait in 1990. But in each case we would have encouraged and empowered an evil enemy. Yet today, there are many who would seek peace by ignoring the evil of global jihad. This is suicidal foolishness.

It is frequently said that we should strive not to be liked but to be respected. But we don't have to choose one or the other. If we seek respect by trying to deserve respect, if we are bold yet judicious in our foreign policy, supporting freedom where we can, that respect will lead to genuine admiration.

When we try to be liked at all costs, we are less deserving of support and admiration. When we stand up for our principles, we earn the respect of the world. There will always be people who don't like us. But if we are doing the right things, that is their problem and not ours.

The world has a population problem.

When I was a kid, the best and the brightest warned of a global threat of apocalyptic dimensions—the "population explosion." The great monument of this hysteria is Paul Ehrlich's 1968 book *The Population Bomb*, which has become a byword for spectacularly inaccurate doomsaying.

If you just look at the figures for world population, they can give pause. There are currently 7.3 billion people walking the planet. But when America was born, there were fewer than one billion. The world reached two billion during the Roaring Twenties, three billion the year John F. Kennedy was elected president (1960). Then it gets eye-popping: four billion the year Nixon resigned (1974), five billion the year of the Robert Bork and Iran-Contra hearings (1987), six billion the year we were freaking out over Y2K (1999), and seven billion just before President Obama's reelection.

That's a lot of people, no doubt. But as we settle into a current pattern of adding about a billion new souls every dozen years, the key question should be: can the Earth accommodate these increases? In terms of acreage, the answer is an emphatic yes. Room is not a problem. But it's not that simple. Expanding populations have to have room to grow fruitfully, with the expectation of sufficient resources to enjoy prosperity. Fortunately, this is exactly what has happened.

This easily accommodated growth might not continue forever. While we have plenty of land for additional people, the planet and its resources are finite. We may reach a point at which the earth says "enough." But we are nowhere close to that now. Every time we have thought we were running out of resources, we have been proved wrong. Remember "peak oil"?

There are areas of the world teeming with suffering people crammed into tight spaces, but the problems there are political. A large population is not a guarantee of strife or poverty. You'll find a lot of people in both Lagos and Manhattan, crowds in both Karachi and Hong Kong. Where there is economic freedom, an educated populace, and wise governance, large populations thrive.

Nicholas Eberstadt of the American Enterprise Institute neatly listed some of the key population myths in a 2011 *Washington Post* article, showing that population density alone is not a problem (Monaco: sixteen thousand people per square kilometer; Bangladesh: one thousand) and that rapid growth does not put the skids on prosperity (noting South Korea and Taiwan, with sharp increases in population and per capita income during the twentieth century).[1]

So even as we recognize that additional decades of population growth are not ruinous, it is worth noting that these rates of increase may not last. By this century's end, we may not have anywhere near the fourteen billion people that recent linear increases might suggest. Childbirth rates are leveling out if not falling in various parts of the world, leading some to suggest that world population growth may slow to the point of reaching a peak, perhaps within a couple of generations.[2]

All such estimates are broad guesses at best. No one knows what will happen to the rates at which we choose to replace ourselves in the coming years. But it is clear that past panics of overpopulation have been as baseless as the climate concerns that have often accompanied them, and that such alarms are often based more in social theory than science.

Appeasing tyrants is a great idea.

The two foremost evils of our time are terrorism and communism. Within a single calendar year, America has found a way to reward both.

The hotly debated Iran nuclear deal, finalized in the summer of 2015, freed up nearly $150 billion in previously frozen Iranian assets, a prize the Iranian regime did virtually nothing to earn. No meaningful inspections were required, no effective barriers to Iran's ballistic missile program were erected, and no restraints were placed on the regime's notorious sponsorship of terror.

The Iranian people are no fools. They took to the streets to celebrate a deal they instantly recognized as a winning lottery ticket acquired at virtually no cost. Faced with criticism of this Iranian slam dunk, Secretary of State John Kerry admitted that some of the freed-up cash "will end up in the hands of the IRGC or other entities, some of which are labeled terrorists."[3]

That would be the Iranian Revolutionary Guard Corps, and the reason they are "labeled" terrorists is because that's what they are. So is the whole government of Iran, to which President Obama chose to hand the keys to the nuclear store, presumably to show us that the nasty old conservative way of dealing with terrorist regimes—namely, opposing them—is so yesterday.

Better to open doors, clasp hands, craft deals and hold press conferences, even if the result endangers America and the Middle East, particularly our ally Israel, which under the deal is far more easily nuked by an emboldened Iranian government that dreams of that day—and does us the occasional favor of telling us so.

Unable to claim progress on the battlefield, Obama and Kerry tried to appear diplomatically successful, reaching agreement for agreement's sake, a far less rigorous course than the heavy lifting of winning a war. But there is a cost to coddling jihadist tyrants, who are encouraged by our enfeeblement.

In April 2016, U.S. Navy ships intercepted Iranian weapons bound for rebels in Yemen. The 1500 AK-47 rifles and two hundred rocket-propelled grenade launchers were intended to help the Houthi rebels who seized the Yemeni capital in 2014 as part of a Shiite partnership to surround Saudi Arabia with pockets of Iranian influence. The Iranian mullahs know their adventures have a good chance of proceeding unchecked at least until the Obama presidency ends. One can only hope their boldness does not extend to additional terrorist toils in the Middle East or any other enclave filled with the Jews and Christians they may seek to convert by the sword.

Meanwhile, if Iran does something that might rankle even Barack Obama, he will be unlikely to stand up to it for fear that the Iranians will walk away from the deal he needs to assert some shred of foreign policy legacy.

This is not a good place to be.

Mere months after the Iran deal stained the history books, the United States reached out to tyrants of a different stripe, the communist Castros of Cuba. The lingering Cold War with Cuba had dragged on long enough, it was said. The time had come for a new approach to the fetid island tyranny.

So with a stroke of Obama's omnipotent pen, U.S. relations with Cuba were "normalized," a curious term, since the norms in Cuba have remained unchanged across the decades of Castro rule—crushing poverty, stifling denials of basic rights, and a perverse ongoing celebration of the totalitarian model we have been trying to defeat for generations.

But sanctions weren't "working," argued the Obama administration. If by that one means the Castros had not yet been overthrown by freedom-starved citizens, then no, they had not worked. Yet. But now there is no reason for the masses to rise up. The cruise ships are already docking, and a torrent of cash and Starbucks locations will follow. This is a massive reward to the nation's communist regime. The Castros have cause for celebration. They have outplayed and outlasted us.

How long did it take to win our freedom from the British crown? How long did it take to win the Cold War? How long will it take to quell global jihad? Big, important worldwide goals often take time.

President Obama was thrilled to bury the "last remnant of the Cold War in the Americas." We can always bring wars to a close by surrendering.

The president must have known that he was prolonging the staying power of the communist regime in Cuba. Either he did not care or other things seemed more important—like the dagger he plunged into the heart of American moral resiliency on the Cuba issue.

Fifty years ago we told Fidel Castro and the people of Cuba that communism would not be tolerated and that the doors to trade and diplomatic relations were closed until the regime changed. That left the ball of freedom in the court of the Cuban people. The day they will taste freedom is now indefinitely delayed.

Standing up to terrorists and communists is always hard and sometimes unpopular. It requires steadfastness and a willingness to stick to the principles that define us. Sadly, resolve and commitment to principle have not been characteristics of American leadership for several years. The evidence is mounting that the policy of bending over to Tehran and Havana isn't working. Reversals will be jarring, but they are necessary.

17

CRIME AND
PUNISHMENT

Poverty causes crime.

There is no doubt that crime occurs disproportionately in America's economically challenged neighborhoods. It is tempting, therefore, to conclude that poverty *causes* crime, a conclusion that fits with the growing tendency to find almost any excuse for bad behavior. That conclusion, however, is both illogical and toxic.

After the riots sparked by the Rodney King verdict in 1992, the *Los Angeles Times* and other media outlets tried to "explain" the criminality that followed a trial with a result some found quite unsatisfactory. Some journalists excused the rioters on the basis of "rage," as if being angry enough entitles crowds to kill, maim, and plunder. But woven through many of the stories was the fiction that people are driven to such lethal excesses by mere economic disadvantage.

If this were true, wouldn't we have seen rampant violence during the Depression years of the 1930s? Of course there were examples of individuals' acting out of desperation, the occasional theft committed to feed a family. But by and large, Depression-era America had something we have lost much of today: a social consensus that denounces rather than excuses crime.

As a child of ten in the suburbs of Washington, I saw portions of the city destroyed by rioters after the assassination of Martin Luther King Jr. My fifth-grade mind could not comprehend the tragedy of his killing, but I also could not grasp why people reacted by destroying their own neighborhoods.

In 1990, after seven more years of school, four years of college, and a decade of radio news and talk show jobs, I returned to Washington to work for a station I had grown up listening to. I knew what Shaw and Columbia Heights had looked like before they were set ablaze, and I had seen them decay further in the decade after the 1968 riots. When I returned as an adult, the Fourteenth Street corridor was still largely a wasteland.

For a conservative talk show host in a liberal city, the question of how a city recovers from such despair proved a rich topic for conversation with my listeners. When I asked them about crime, I'd hear about the desperation of poverty. What exactly is it about economic struggle, I asked, that causes people to commit crime? I had seen a lot of poverty everywhere I had lived and worked, and there were countless people living in it who didn't fall into violence, drugs, or other crimes.

What do those people have in common? Character. Our inner cities teem with lawbreakers, but among them are family members, mentors, and church leaders who are in the same economic plight but who have made better decisions in life. Those decisions, and not mere financial factors, determine whether a life is spent obeying laws or breaking them.

Police are eager to abuse minorities.

A lie, if told often enough, will eventually be accepted as truth. This insight is often attributed to Hitler or his propaganda minister, Joseph Goebbels, but it appears to have a less sinister origin. William James (1842–1910), considered one of the founders of modern psychology, observed, "There's nothing so absurd that if you repeat it often enough, people will believe it."

The latest vindication of that principle is the malicious untruth that the police are out to kill black people. Have we seen some dubious police killings? Yes, and they will happen on occasion. Have we seen some shootings that were obviously unjustified from the start? Yes, and we have not seen the last of them, not with every phone-toting witness a photojournalist. That technology is a good thing; genuine accountability is what we want.

But how did we get to the point where an entire movement proclaims that "Black Lives Matter," as if the data suggest that they do not? Where the film director Quentin Tarantino, referring to the police, declares to a crowd, "I have to call a murder a murder, and I have to call the murderers the murderers"? We are all on the side of the murdered. But we should not be on the side of a mob that indiscriminately maligns police officers. Maybe we should be on the side of the facts.

Data on arrest-related deaths between 2003 and 2009 published by the Bureau of Justice Statistics show that 4,813 suspects died during or shortly after arrest or restraint.[1] If that number seems high, consider that there were ninety-eight million arrests during that period, making the fatality rate less than .005 percent.

In light of the rarity of such killings, the evidence that the cops have placed a bounty on the heads of black citizens is less compelling. An exhaustive analysis by the *Washington Post* of the 965 fatal shootings by police in the United States in 2015 found that less than 4 percent of those shootings involved unarmed black men and white cops.[2] Hidden in those numbers are the various factors that can lead to a policeman's split-second decision to fire. The *Post* quoted the president of the Pennsylvania Fraternal Order of Police, Les Neri, who lamented how the frame-by-frame analysis of some videos can obscure the circumstances in which officers must act: "We now microscopically evaluate for days and weeks what they only had a few seconds to act on. People say 'They shot an unarmed man,' but we know that only after the fact. We are criminalizing judgment errors."

Richard Johnson, a criminologist at the University of Toledo, examined data from the FBI and the Centers for Disease Control for 2003–2012, reaching conclusions that Deroy Murdock reported in the *New York Post*:

> On average, 4,472 black men were killed by other black men annually between Jan. 1, 2009, and Dec. 31, 2012, according to the FBI's Supplementary Homicide Reports. Using FBI and CDC statistics, Professor Johnson calculates that 112 black men, on average, suffered both justified and unjustified police-involved deaths annually during this period. This equals 2.5 percent of these 4,472 yearly deaths. For every black man—criminal or innocent—killed by a cop, 40 black men were murdered by other black men. The, at most, 2.5 percent of the problem generates relentless rage. And, yet, it is rude-to-racist to mention 97.5 percent of the problem.[3]

As with so many intentional misstatements, the fraud of a predatory police force is a distraction from an uncomfortable truth—in this case, the tragedy of rampant crime featuring black victims and black perpetrators. People of all colors want real accountability in cases of police misbehavior. No good is served in burying the valid cases that deserve our attention under a mountain of fictitious race-baiting.

America has too many prisons.

The complaint is frequent: America has too many people in jail. You may hear that we have only 5 percent of the world's population but 25 percent of its prisoners. Those statistics are correct, but maybe the explanation is that we simply do a better job of incarcerating lawbreakers than other countries do.

Crime is hardly a rarity in America, and a country that doesn't lock up its criminals quickly becomes a violent hellhole. So is it possible that our large prison population is a justifiable result of a growing crime problem, and that locking up more people who deserve to be locked up has made us safer?

This explanation runs afoul of the popular myth of "mass incarceration," but the facts support it. The *Wall Street Journal* reported that crime in America skyrocketed 350 percent between 1960 and 1990. Debunking the fantasy that our jails are filled with kids unlucky enough to get caught doing drugs for their own personal jollies, it also reported that 75 percent of the people doing time for drugs are dealers, not users. In federal facilities, nearly all drug inmates are dealers.[4]

In the last twenty years, violent crime has dropped as our prison population swelled. Violent offenders on the streets make for dangerous communities. Jailing them makes those communities safer. What a concept!

Racial activists suggest that our justice system is purposefully looking for innocent minorities to incarcerate. Even if we stipulate that our humanly flawed system may not provide perfect justice for all races, the reason for minorities' disproportionate presence behind bars is their disproportionate tendency to commit crimes.

Across all racial and socioeconomic barriers, people are in prison because they deserve to be there. When our prison population was smaller, we had more crime. Now we have larger prison numbers and lower crime numbers. What's wrong with that?

Perhaps we are riding a cycle that will lead to fewer people deserving incarceration. That would be great. So are various initiatives that identify some crimes that do not necessarily need to lead to prison, especially for juveniles. But for the most part, prison is the correct response to serious violations of the law. If our crime problem continues to wane, as we should all desire, let's make sure we don't turn all of those prisons into condos just yet. That next wave of soft-on-crime politicians is always just an election away, their heads filled with policies that could well facilitate a new burst of crime.

18

GUNS

America's gun culture is a problem.

People rarely talk about the "gun culture" with approval. A Google search of the term brings up endless laments about the horrible guns owned by Americans, blaming gun violence on an inanimate object rather than the people who commit gun crime.

Having been around guns and gun owners all of my life, the "gun culture" I know is devoted to self-protection and safe sportsmanship. And while not all gun owners are conservative, a passion for gun rights is highly correlated with a deep appreciation for the Bill of Rights.

As our nation grew, millions of Americans were equipped with the guns that enabled them to feed and protect their families. So what changed? Human behavior. We have always had guns, but we did not have epidemics of gun crime until our social fabric began to tear. Malevolent people will misuse guns when they're available, but when they do, whose fault is it? The gun's, which is the same object in the hand of a cop or a criminal, a soldier or a mass shooter? Or is it a people problem?

America has a gun culture, but it is the health of our general culture that will determine whether we have a gun crime problem. Pointing to nations with no comparable tradition of gun ownership or less social strife is useless. Guns will continue to be a part of American life, and the evidence suggests that's a good thing. John Lott's 1998 masterpiece, *More Guns, Less Crime*, dismantled the case for disarming law-abiding citizens. In 2013, President Obama's own Justice Department released statistics showing gun-related homicides dropping nearly 40 percent from 1993 to 2011. Non-lethal gun crimes dropped even more, nearly 70 percent.[1]

A reduction in gun crime is wonderful news. What a shame that gun-demonizers drowned it out with their misplaced aggression. A Pew Research survey that year revealed an American public grossly unaware of the truth of gun crime, 56 percent believing it had risen in the previous twenty years, and only 12 percent responding correctly that it had fallen.[2] Say what you will about panic-mongering; it often works.

In *Forbes* that year, Larry Bell asked whether it was time for universal recognition that Professor Lott's conclusions were correct:

> Gwainevere Catchings Hess, president of the Black Women's Agenda (BWA), Inc., an organization that strongly advocates strict gun-control legislation, rightly points out that "*In 2009, black males ages 15–19 were eight times as likely as white males the same age, and 2.5 times as likely as their Hispanic peers to be killed in a gun homicide.*"

Those are terrible statistics, but here are some others. Today, 72% of black children are born out of wedlock, as are 53% of Hispanic children and 36% of white children. Back in 1965, 25% of black children were born out of wedlock, nearly one-third fewer. As a result, promiscuous rappers, prosperous dope peddlers and street gang leaders are becoming ever more influential role models. It's probably no big stretch of imagination to correlate such grossly disproportionate crime and victimization rates with comparably staggering rates of single-parent families, those without fathers in particular.[3]

If "gun culture" is the sum of what Americans do with their guns, its positives vastly outweigh the negatives. Violence is not the result of the mere proliferation of guns but of our social pathologies.

Gun control will curtail mass killings.

The hours following a mass shooting bring a wave of horror and grief. News channels devote hours to the story, their anchors and reporters struggling to fill long stretches of air time without a shred of new information.

I feel for these folks. They can't break away for other stories while their competition scrapes and scours for tidbits about shooters and victims. But as the public prays and reaches out to the afflicted community, journalists predictably turn to what have become conventional narratives.

Some people, not all of them conservative, recognize that virtually all of these tragedies involve tortured souls who have sent distress signals of one sort or another before making their final, lethal move.

Sometimes it's a jihadist. Other times the story begins with a mentally ill person unable to cope with the world around him. But whether committed by terrorists or psychopaths, shootings are behavioral problems.

There is a natural inclination to address the behavioral and psychological malfunctions that lead to gun violence. How can we recognize potentially dangerous persons? How might we help them? What procedures might protect us from such acts? All good questions.

Then there are the people who want to take our guns away.

Gun control advocates can talk a good game about appreciating the Second Amendment, understanding the interests of hunters and target shooters and seeking measures that leave our rights intact. Do not believe this fraud for a moment. They want to make it harder for law-abiding people to acquire guns and ammo, believing that such laws will actually stop a maniac from perpetrating the next massacre.

In 2008, presidential candidate Hillary Clinton calculated that her designs on other people's firearms would not play so well in states like Pennsylvania, Indiana, Kentucky, and West Virginia, where even the Democrats shoot every once in a while. So she tried to distance herself from her opponent Barack Obama's disparaging comment about voters who "cling to guns or religion or antipathy to people who aren't like them."

"I disagree with Senator Obama's assertion that people in our country cling to guns," she told supporters in Valparaiso, Indiana. "It's part of culture. It's part of a way of life. People enjoy hunting and shooting because it's an important part of who they are. Not because they are bitter."

Nice. But it's deeds, not words, that count. Mrs. Clinton and other gun-grabbers can pay lip service to recreational gun use all they like. Some of them even mean it. But the Second Amendment was not adopted to protect hunting. It was adopted to protect citizens from tyranny. At this point, we are still more likely to be threatened by criminal thugs than by federal storm troopers. But that same amendment gives us the right to protect ourselves from anything that may ever endanger us. Or we can go shoot deer. It's our call. It's our freedom. Those are our guns.

But that drives some people crazy. In their ideological frenzy, they have misled the public into thinking gun violence is getting worse, persuading many that gun control is a sensible measure. It is not. But even as the evidence mounts against them, these zealots can be counted on to cling to their gun control positions.

Lucidity does break through from time to time. In the wake of the San Bernardino terrorist massacre in December 2015, with the Obama White House leading the usual gun-blaming chorus, Jonathan Karl of ABC asked the White House press secretary, Josh Earnest, "Did [the president] have any indication at that point that, if Congress instituted stronger background checks, it would have prevented this incident?"

"In this incident, of course not," Earnest replied, raising eyebrows. Reverting to partisanship, however, the loyal spokesman continued, "But the president is confident, and I think common-sense-thinking Americans are confident, that if there are things that Congress can do to make it harder for individuals who shouldn't have guns from getting them, then Congress should act and pass a law accordingly, because that law can be implemented in a way that doesn't undermine the constitutional rights of law-abiding Americans."

He should have stopped after "of course not."

Real solutions to gun crime are hard. They require the political will to severely punish gun-related offenses and a plan for profiling potential mass shooters. We can't lock people up for what we think they might do, and being a reclusive oddball is not a crime. But mental health professionals and lawmakers are having conversations about how to support friends and family members who seek help for their alarmingly troubled loved ones. At some point, those conversations will necessarily turn toward involuntary commitments to mental health facilities, a thorny issue fraught with hazards.

It's easier just to grab the guns, a tempting expedient for politicians who want credit for "doing something" about the problem. But few problems are alleviated by rank opportunism.

Failure to enact gun control equals "complacency."

The campaign to infringe on gun rights necessarily includes attacks on those unwilling to lie down for such mischief. Americans refusing to use shootings as an occasion to disarm the law-abiding are the target of invective that starts at the top—the White House. President Obama assures us that all he wants is "common sense" gun safety laws—the implication being that to oppose him is to oppose common sense.

The routine is now familiar. First, there is a shooting somewhere. Second, the Left calls for gun control to stem future shootings. Third, dissenting voices respond that gun control is as ineffective as it is unconstitutional. A multi-layered offensive follows. Defenders of gun rights are "complacent" about gun violence. Then someone plays the "one life" card—"if we can save just one life, wouldn't it be worth it?"

Well, no. We all want to save lives, but not in ways that are an assault on both freedom and logic. We could save at least one life by requiring all drivers to wear full body armor. We could save a life here and there by allowing airlines to fly only in the daytime. We don't order society according to the "one life" principle.

Calling gun-rights advocates "complacent" is a typical leftist tactic to discredit opponents rather than engage them on the facts. Every American wants to find a way to reduce gun violence. The ones who say they want to reach that goal with useless laws are welcome to make their case. The moment they attack the other side as somehow tolerant of the death toll is the moment they reveal the vacuity of their argument.

Concealed carry laws are dangerous.

From 2007 to 2014, violent crime in the United States dropped by 22 percent. It is worth noting that concealed carry permits soared by 146 percent in the same period.[4] Murder and violent crime rates are also lower in the twenty-five states with the highest permit rates. Several factors may be at work, but the charge that concealed carry is a path to wild-west carnage has been thoroughly discredited.

In 1976, Governor Zell Miller secured the passage of a trailblazing concealed carry law in Georgia, and other states followed in the ensuing decade. In the late 1980s, Florida was the stage for a fight over concealed carry. Its opponents warned of a bloodbath, ignoring the most compelling argument for concealed carry—that the additional guns in our midst are carried by some of our most upstanding, law-abiding citizens. When no disasters followed Florida's new law, the floodgates were opened, and today all fifty states permit some form of concealed carry.

Those who still fear guns in the hands of good people should consider a story that led to the passage of concealed carry in my state of Texas. In 1991, Suzanna Gratia-Hupp was eating with her parents at a Luby's restaurant in Killeen when George Hennard drove his pickup through the plate glass window and shot twenty-three people dead, including Suzanna's parents, before killing himself. As the bullets flew, Suzanna reached instinctively for the pistol she carried in her purse. But obeying the law that banned her gun from the restaurant, she had left it in her car. She became the face of the concealed carry movement in Texas.

We don't know if Suzanna could have saved her parents or any of the other victims in what was then the deadliest mass shooting in U.S. history. But in two of the subsequent shootings with larger death tolls (Virginia Tech with thirty-two in 2007, Sandy Hook with twenty-six in 2012), the absence of good people with guns ensured the lethal success of the bad people with guns. Nightclubs like Pulse in Orlando do not attract a gun-toting clientele, but the presence there of armed citizens in the wee hours of June 13, 2016, might have cut short the deadliest mass shooting in U.S. history. We should seriously revisit the wisdom of any establishment's choice to force customers to shed the weapons that could save lives.

Suzanna Gratia-Hupp eventually served ten years in the Texas legislature, where she was an enduring example of the added security concealed carry can provide. The truth of concealed carry laws is that they do indeed pose a danger—to criminals.

19

DRUGS

Addiction is not a matter of personal responsibility.

Addicts are a diverse community. Addiction knows no sex, no race, no social class. There are rich and poor alcoholics, junkies under bridges and in mansions.

But there's also a diversity to be found among people who have beaten their addictions, and plenty who have not—they are not of one mind when it comes to whether they are to blame for their predicament. Not their addiction, their predicament. The addiction itself may be a horrible hand dealt to them by heredity or environment. But what one does with that hand is very much a matter of choice.

For all the voices preaching that addiction is a disease as unbeatable as an aggressive cancer, I have spoken to few addicts who wish to cash in that free pass. Granted, many are alcoholics who have completed the twelve steps of Alcoholics Anonymous or drug users who have found the Lord and with him sobriety. But their stories have a common element: they may not know what led them into addiction, but they know full well whose job it was to get them out.

Some try to minimize a person's responsibility to extract himself from addiction's clutches, and there are others who will scold any addict for not gutting up and getting clean. Neither approach is useful. There is surely a degree of personal responsibility for drug and alcohol abuse, even if one has some mysterious wiring that makes it very hard to stop. Millions have kicked their habits, proving that it can be done. But it is clearly one of the hardest things imaginable. We have all heard stories of lives ravaged by addiction, then healed by rehab or a spiritual epiphany or just a simple moment of clarity amid the wreckage. Then just when relief sets in, the destructive behavior returns. A man who served ten years in prison for drug offenses, was released, busted again, jailed for five more years, and then released again told me after years of subsequent sobriety, "You never really cure addiction; you just outrun it."

Placing some level of responsibility on the addict is not a disservice. People who have licked their addictions have a common trait— they reached a moment when they said "No more." They then took action to change their lives. Some did it through the AA method of confessing powerlessness and surrendering to a higher power; others simply looked in the mirror and summoned the will to change their lives. But they all had The Moment.

That moment is an inspiring example of human strength of will. It may seem counterintuitive, but even an admission of powerlessness is a moment of strength. It shows clarity, reason, and willingness to change. Addiction can surely have deep roots in brain chemistry, but that doesn't mean it is an irrevocable sentence. Asserting a moral component does not mean branding addicts as immoral—we all struggle with making decisions that are good and bad for our lives. Addicts swim against a strong tide of destructive urges. They deserve prayerful support and understanding.

It is not "shaming" to remind addicts that the path away from addiction is available to them by their own choices. Many discussions treat the issue as binary, either wholly a treatable disease or a moral issue. It is both. Addiction can be treated, but unlike most diseases, it usually becomes a problem because of what the addict has done, and can be dealt with most effectively when the addict decides to change his behavior. No treatment can succeed without the decision to avoid drugs or alcohol, which is—since it involves doing what is right or wrong for addicts and those around them—a moral decision.

Legalizing pot is a great idea.

At the end of the turbulent 1960s, only 12 percent of Americans favored the legalization of marijuana, with 84 percent opposed.[1] Ah, the good old days.

In the last couple of years, the lines tracking those views crossed. The path to majority support for legalization was not straight. As the 1980s began, 30 percent were in favor; as the decade ended, perhaps after years of Nancy Reagan's maligned but ultimately sublime "Just Say No" message, support had fallen to 16 percent.

The 1990s ushered in the era of presidents who had rolled a joint or two, whether inhaling or not. Approval for pot legalization jumped back above 30 percent. The path toward majority approval has been predictably marked by laws in more than a dozen states decriminalizing pot, and outright legalization in four states and the District of Columbia.

So how's that working out?

Great, if you smoke. Among those who don't, opinions vary from approval on libertarian grounds, ambivalence, or objections based on principle or just noticing what legalization has wrought.

Before full legalization took effect in Colorado, the columnist Linda Chavez braced for the consequences:

> Even before marijuana becomes legal, the effects of the drug are apparent in everyday life in the city I now call home. The work ethic in Boulder already leaves something to be desired. Try finding someone to put in a full eight-hour day doing home repair, painting or yard work in this college town. If they show up by 10, you're lucky—and don't be surprised if their eyes are a little bloodshot after lunch and they knock off work by 3. I imagine it only will get worse once pot is legal.
>
> My dad painted houses for a living. He was always on the job by 8 a.m. and stayed until it was too dark to work or the job was finished. The only people with similar work habits now seem to be immigrants—who, according to the National Survey on Drug Use and Health, use marijuana at less than half the rate of American-born adults.[2]

So have Ms. Chavez's concerns played out? Just five months into the legal pot experiment, the thoroughly pot-approving *New York Times* noted, "Despite a galaxy of legal, regulated marijuana stores across the state, prosecutors say a dangerous illicit market persists."[3] Imagine that. But didn't the pro-pot activists promise legalization would bring all the pot sales out into the sunshine, where the black markets that were the product of "prohibition" would evaporate?

There were other things the cannabis cheering section did not foresee, like kids snarfing Grandma's suddenly available weed brownies. When the smokables became legal, the much harder to identify edibles did too, and emergency rooms are seeing the effects.

The same *New York Times* article noted the Colorado State Patrol's tracking of motorists impaired by marijuana. One out of every eight citations is for driving stoned. Throw in legal pot's being hustled out of state, and you have a portrait of a state weathering the various downsides of a bad law.

The most obvious lie about legal pot is that usage would not go up appreciably. In every state opening the Pandora's box of legal marijuana, countless citizens will see the only barrier to their usage evaporate. Millions of Americans refrain from smoking pot for only one reason—it's illegal.

It's easy to understand the libertarian argument that people should be able to do whatever they wish as long as the rights of others are not violated. But what about the right to pass laws that protect safety and quality of life? There is no constitutional right to a bong hit. For years I've been asking callers to my radio show a question that no one has answered successfully: Is there one way in which the legalization of additional intoxicants makes society better?

The war on drugs isn't working.

Our libertarian friends are right about so many things, but on one of their favorite issues, they've got it wrong—the "failed" war on drugs. By what measure has it failed? That we still have drug use? The high cost of enforcing laws? The stigma imposed on otherwise law-abiding people? Those are their favorite selling points. They all fail.

Yes, we still have drug use. And we still have robbery, assault, and speeding despite laws against them. It's a universal truth that we get more of what we legalize and less of what we prohibit. Suppose that for every crime for which someone was arrested, another person got away with it. Would that constitute an argument for abolishing those laws because they "failed"? How about speed limits? People speed every day, usually without getting caught. But enforcement reduces the number of speeders because most of us do not want to get caught.

Drug laws are expensive to enforce. All laws are expensive to enforce. The expenditure is either worth it or not. It will never appear justified to people who resent the laws in the first place. I, for one, am pleased to tell my teenage son that among the reasons he should stay away from drugs is that they are illegal. Illegality is a societal statement that "we believe people should not be doing this." What a tragedy for parents to lose having the law on their side.

As for the stain of criminality that a drug conviction will leave on a defendant who has broken no other laws, isn't that true for any other one-time lawbreaker? This is the argument of people who don't believe drug violations are "real" crimes. Of course there is a difference between a dumb guy caught with a joint in his pocket and a narcotics kingpin. That's why the sentences are different. And maybe we need smarter sentencing so that a nineteen-year-old doesn't spend a decade in jail for growing a pot plant in his dorm room. But the war on drugs works every time someone decides not to use or sell drugs for fear of being caught. That happens countless times a day.

Ending the war on drugs will release numerous people from prison who have demonstrated their willingness to break the law. Others with that same proclivity will be less likely to be incarcerated. The motivation for this folly often hinges on some strain of racial sensitivity, since minorities are overrepresented in our prison populations. But leniency doesn't help the black and Hispanic Americans who are also disproportionate *victims* of crime, their neighborhoods poisoned by the drug culture. Anyone calling for an end to the drug war should think about the effects of letting drug offenders wander those neighborhoods.

Leaders in both parties gravitate toward softening drug laws because they think it curries favor with a growing national mood. Sadly, they may be right.

20

CLIMATE

The science is settled: man is changing the earth's temperature.

When an argument begins to collapse, the people clinging to it may attempt to proclaim that the matter is settled. This has become the favored tactic of climate alarmists. As resistance mounts among scientists and other clear-headed people, there is an air of panic in the movement.

Increasingly shrill crusaders are telling us that climate change is not just a problem, it's our *biggest* problem—more daunting than terrorism or the national debt.

No one in the growing insurgency against this nonsense should suggest that we somehow know mankind is *not* having a climatic effect on the planet. That is exactly the point: It is impossible to know whether human industriousness is causing global warming. We can't even get together on whether the planet is even warming anymore.

We're told that there is an overwhelming consensus on climate change among the world's scientists. But as Galileo would tell us, science does not progress by defending the consensus. Consensus is made to be challenged.

If we stipulate for the sake of argument that global temperatures are indeed rising, how do we know that man's activity is responsible? Credentialed climate scientists say they know we are warming the planet. A growing number of equally credentialed skeptics are pushing back. But the dissenters are not asserting that man has no role in climate change; they're simply calling for intellectual modesty in the face of woefully incomplete data.

We have accurately measured temperatures for only a couple of centuries, and our extrapolations into the past are not nearly as precise as current measurements. ("Paleoclimatologists" are fond of poking through tree rings and ice core layers as if they were old almanacs). But within the window of scientific acuity, we have seen the planet warm, and we have seen it cool—even within a single lifetime.

In the mid-1970s, after man had been pumping pollutants into the atmosphere for decades, the planet's temperature was actually dropping. A now-famous *Newsweek* article ("The Cooling World," April 28, 1975) cited "ominous signs that the Earth's weather patterns have begun to change dramatically, and that these changes may portend a drastic decline in food production." The article cited the "almost unanimous" opinion of meteorologists that chilly temperatures would endanger worldwide agriculture.

In the ensuing decades, as it appeared that the planet was warming up instead, Chicken Littles emerged from climate labs and Hollywood movie sets, clucking that major coastal cities would soon be under water and forlorn polar bears would find nary an ice floe to perch upon.

What changed? Politics and the money connected to it. Liberal politicians began warning of doomsday if we failed to muzzle the industries that had fallen out of their favor, primarily those producing or burning fossil fuels. The Left seethed with resentment at Americans' driving what they wanted when they wanted. Science, like everything else, got politicized.

Climate change is real, of course. The climate does change. What is open to question is whether smokestacks and SUVs are nudging the planet's temperature upward. One would think the planet would have turned red hot after the two centuries of uninhibited industrialization before the environmental movement of the 1960s and the technology that gave us cleaner factories, cleaner energy, and cleaner cars.

Attempts to connect human enterprise to planetary warming are prone to the fallacy known as *post hoc, ergo propter hoc*—the assumption that because B follows A, B is caused by A. The earth's temperature has gone up and it has gone down over the centuries. To conclude that the increases are the result of human activity is an offense not just to science but to basic logic.

Today's weather patterns are uniquely alarming.

One of the reasons "global warming" has given way to "climate change" as the preferred slogan is that the planet may not be warming so much lately—a development that could force the movement to fold up its revival tents and find something else to worry about. "Climate change" is so vague a term that it encompasses almost *anything*: floods and droughts, bursts of storm activity, abnormal warmth *and* abnormal cold.

I have had to fend off conspiratorial notions of why stories of turbulent weather lead off so many network newscasts. Weather extremes are a fact of life. There is nothing exceptional about the current patterns of storm activity. We have droughts; we have floods; we have cold snaps; we have warm spurts. It's what planets do. But if the media can score a double bonus—striking imagery of hurricane damage coupled with the politically satisfying charge that we are causing it—that has to be pretty tempting.

Hurricanes are in the news so often not because there are more of them but because so many Americans are choosing to live where they hit. If a family from the frozen tundra of the upper Midwest decides to take its chances in the breezy coastal South, I can understand, but more people will be in the path of the next hurricane. Patrick J. Michaels, a research professor of environmental sciences at the University of Virginia, has found that ninety-seven hurricanes hit the United States from 1901 to 1950, while only seventy-two hit in the half-century that followed.[1] The notion that man-made climate change is responsible for more hurricanes is a double-barreled fraud, combining the assertion that hurricanes are more frequent with the certainty that we made it happen.

The past several years have been tough for the High Priest of the Church of Climate Panic, former Vice President Al Gore. After a screening of his absurd documentary *An Inconvenient Truth* in 2006, he told fawning reporters at the Sundance Film Festival that we would reach a "point of no return" within ten years if we did not adopt drastic measures to curb greenhouse gases.[2] Those ten years have passed, and Gore's imagined cataclysm has been revealed as a hoax.

With past claims of climate catastrophe withering on the vine, provocateurs are left with few tools to startle the masses. Since weather stories always supply useful imagery, look for the alarmists to suggest that storms/floods/droughts/heat waves/locusts/whatever are worse than ever before.

They are lying.

We must take drastic action to fend off climate disasters.

If the basis for climate scare tactics has been eroded, surely there is little foundation for the draconian, economy-crushing solutions sought by the dealers in such deceptions.

You would think.

But climate change activism has never really been about the planet. The proposed solutions align neatly with the economic and social agenda of the Left—less economic freedom, choking off cheap fossil fuels, coerced urban living and mass transit, and always more power in the hands of government and less for the individual citizen.

Don't take my word for it. Christiana Figueres, the executive secretary of the United Nations Framework Convention on Climate Change, let the cat out of the bag at a news conference in February 2015: "This is the first time in the history of mankind that we are setting ourselves the task of intentionally, within a defined period of time, to change the economic development model that has been reigning for at least 150 years, since the Industrial Revolution." Looking forward to the Paris climate conference later that year, she gave voice to her dream: "This is probably the most difficult task we have ever given ourselves, which is to intentionally transform the economic development model for the first time in human history."[3]

Hmm. One hundred fifty years. Sound like the life span of American-led capitalism? There is nothing dishonorable about staking a claim on the far side of environmental protectionism. (Unwise, but not dishonorable.) But those shouldering the climate-change battering ram are motivated less by the fate of the planet than by the opportunity to obliterate capitalism, which has sullied the reputation of their favored structure, authoritarian redistribution.

The Christina Figuereses of the world will tell you that they seek what is right for the poor, yet their policies exact a savage toll on them around the world. Struggling families on every continent face a steeper climb to prosperity if energy prices are artificially boosted by climate control policies. The fossil fuels that built our own prosperity are denied to emerging economies because of disincentives from the supposedly enlightened nations offering aid, but favoring less reliable and costlier alternative energy.

Oh, and we cram corn into our cars.

The ethanol boondoggle is one of the dumbest exploits in the climate change manual. It is bad for cars, bad for the environment, and bad for food prices. If cars ran better with corn or candy bars or any other food product whipped into our gasoline, the marketplace would smile on that, and we would all be using it, not because government wants us to, but because we want to.

There should never be any subsidy for energy. Let people use what they wish to run their cars, heat their homes, and power their lives. Environmentally friendly alternative fuels are a growing industry that does not need a dime of taxpayer help. Our streets hum with hybrid and electric cars, solar panels cover roofs, wind turbines dot increasing spreads of our acreage. These technologies deserve all the success that comes from actual approval by the consuming public.

But from cars to light bulbs, our choices are impeded by climate know-it-alls pushing us toward their approved decisions. And again, love of the earth is not the motivator; it is lust for power, coupled with the worst strain of crony capitalism.

So here's a crazy idea. Let's continue to welcome every green technology we can find that works. Not because someone thinks our grandkids will visit an underwater Times Square, but because it is the right thing to do. We are a virtuous people. We can be trusted to be good stewards of at least our portion of the planet. Perhaps that example will take hold in the exploding economies of India and China, where American environmental busybodies don't seem to mind the abuses as much, because they do not seek to stick their noses into the lives of people in Beijing and Mumbai.

A *warmer planet is bad.*

Let's assume for the sake of argument that the earth is getting a tiny bit warmer. Even if it is not warming now, it will eventually, because temperatures are cyclical. The polar ice caps on Mars are shrinking, and I don't believe any of our unmanned landers have yet photographed a coal-fired plant atop Olympus Mons.

Isn't any change in temperature an advantage in some ways and a disadvantage in others? When temperatures go down, glaciers stabilize, but the amount of land on which we can grow food might shrink. We've been force-fed the horror stories of a warmer planet, but wouldn't that also mean a few extra latitude lines of farmable land? And maybe, heaven forbid, a tiny bit of sting taken from the horribly unlivable winters suffered by millions of Americans and far more in other nations?

Climate change is a fact of life. Man-made climate change is a product of liberal wishful thinking, made more pernicious by its adoption through the years by corruptible scientists. That seems to be changing, as more voices emerge from the skeptical wings of the science community, a development ignored by those who say the "debate is over."

It is often true that those insisting most loudly that a debate is over are the ones who are concerned that it is in fact just beginning.

That concern can even lead to the kind of wounded-animal aggressiveness on display in March 2016 as Attorney General Loretta Lynch admitted to a Senate hearing that her Department of Justice has discussed criminalizing so-called "climate change deniers." (The echo of "Holocaust denier" is no doubt intentional.)

Lynch was responding to a question from Democratic Senator Sheldon Whitehouse of Rhode Island, eager to hear of her pursuit of the "climate denial scheme." Comparisons were made to tobacco industry efforts to obfuscate the risks of smoking. But climate projections are not a representation of known fact. They are speculative. "This matter has been discussed," she revealed. "We have received information about it and have referred it to the FBI to consider whether or not it meets the criteria for which we could take action."

This should scare the hell out of every American. The notion of federal law enforcement cracking down on one side of an ongoing debate is an offense against core American values. The administration that seeks to silence your opponents today could give way to one that would silence you in the future.

21

DEFENDING OUR NATION

NSA surveillance is a gross violation of privacy.

Not every remedy offered in these pages involves trading liberalism for conservatism. Float the topic of National Security Agency surveillance in a room filled with conservatives, and you'll get fiery discord among people who might agree on everything else. In one corner, you'll find the view that Edward Snowden should be revered, in another the view that he should be shot.

Conservatives with some libertarian nucleotides in their DNA have no use for intelligence-gathering that involves compiling metadata pertaining to our private conversations. But I'm grateful for it every day.

The intel analysts working to prevent the next 9/11 are not eavesdropping on your chats with Uncle Ralph; they are heroes. The dots they're connecting are indications of calls made and received. If the origin or destination of a call is suspicious, then and only then does a process begin that might lead to judicial authorization of an investigation of the content of a communication. Otherwise, individuals are not identified.

Enter the Rand Paul armies, insisting that such analysis requires a warrant from the get-go. Senator Paul is heroically faithful to the Constitution, but he is mistaken about the Fourth Amendment. Warrants are required when the government seeks to examine your "person, house, papers and effects"—that is, things that are *yours*. The information that a call was made is not your personal property. It is a business record that is the property of the telecom company, enabling it to, among other things, bill us. Many people whom I respect greatly are wrongly proclaiming that this metadata collection is "spying on the American people." And unfortunately, people who aren't paying close attention have been needlessly unnerved.

Remember what everyone said after 9/11? "We have to be able to connect the dots to prevent such things in the future." What do people think the dots are? They are the nameless, faceless granules of information that can indicate that something foul is afoot. We discard this tool at our peril.

It is easy to understand some level of concern. The Obama administration has squandered what was left of the public's trust in government, using the Internal Revenue Service as a political weapon, turning the vast federal regulatory apparatus into an instrument of tyranny, and musing publicly about subjecting its ideological opponents to criminal prosecution.

I get it. But there is no evidence that our intelligence officials have been corrupted, even by the Obama White House. We have to watch the political hacks—Exhibit A: Janet Napolitano's 2009 Homeland Security report urging vigilance against "right wing extremism," a category that includes "opposition to abortion or immigration"—but there is no reason to think the NSA and CIA have been parties to such shenanigans.

Where is the Rosa Parks of NSA surveillance? Where are the people whose lives have been disrupted by nosy agents on a false premise of national security? Congressional hearings featured a long list of witnesses whom the IRS had punished for their conservatism. If there were any such a victims of the NSA, you can bet your life that libertarians and liberals would join forces to turn them into anti-surveillance poster children. The absence of such heroes for their cause is telling.

The balance between liberty and security is precarious. We should not tolerate real violations of our constitutional rights for the sake of safety. Since 9/11, you often hear that the government's first job is to "keep us safe." Not true. The government's main job is to protect our liberties, guarding our safety within that construct. If an NSA analyst ever used information improperly obtained, we should respond as we would if a police officer had strayed from the law. But just as you don't shut down the police department because of one bad cop, you don't dismantle the surveillance that is our first line of defense in a dangerous world.

Gays in the military are not a problem.

Have gays served honorably in the armed forces? They have. Is the pendulum swinging toward acceptance of homosexuality? It is. Does basic human decency require that gays be treated fairly? It does. So is homosexuality in the military a good idea? It is not. Follow carefully.

The job of the United States military is to maintain a fighting force that can win wars as quickly and efficiently as possible. Anything that impedes that job is a bad idea. While we may appreciate any gays who have served our nation dutifully, we must examine whether it is a good idea for them to have been there in the first place.

"Unit cohesion" has been derided as homophobic code language, a useful tool for banning gays just for the sake of it. But the term means something. It's what a fighting force must have for utmost readiness. The 1992 report of the Presidential Commission on the Assignment of Women in the Armed Forces provides a useful definition, one that was not formulated with homosexuality in mind:

> Cohesion is the relationship that develops in a unit or group where
> a. members share common values and experiences
> b. individuals in the group conform to group norms and behavior in order to ensure group survival and goals
> c. members lose their personal identity in favor of a group identity
> d. members focus on group activities and goals
> e. unit members become totally dependent on each other for the completion of their mission or survival, and
> f. group members must meet all standards of performance and behavior in order not to threaten group survival.
> Cohesion can be negatively affected by the introduction of any element that detracts from the need for such key ingredients as mutual confidence, commonality of experience, and equitable treatment.[1]

Advocates of homosexuality in uniform rightly object to the image of gay soldiers on the prowl for that next relationship, but the mere prospect of sexual attraction within a combat unit is a deal-breaker. It is not homophobic for a straight soldier to recoil at the thought of being sexually attractive to a comrade in the uniquely intimate conditions of combat duty. This is something our fighting forces should never have to worry about, and if that means exclusion of a few willing, committed, and patriotic gay Americans, that's what we have to do.

Why? Because no one has a right to be in the military. The terms of its service are properly defined by law in whatever way best serves the nation's interests. In this context, sexual segregation cannot be compared to racial segregation. Racial differences are wholly irrelevant to the military's mission. Sexuality is at the core of our identity as people. While there are many places where sexual orientation is irrelevant, military service is not one of them.

And for the record, "Don't Ask, Don't Tell" was always nonsense. If homosexuality in the service is a good idea, telling is not a problem. And if it is not, asking is not a problem.

Well, it is not a good idea. And if you've heard of nations lifting their "gay bans" with no adverse effects, I would suggest that the Netherlands and Scandinavia are not doing the heavy lifting in the world's hot zones these days. The Israeli Defense Forces, which surely have their hands full, have allowed open homosexuality since 1993, but not in ground combat or intelligence units.[2] Gay soldiers are permitted to shower alone, a lovely nod to privacy but inefficient on the battlefield. And while the IDF is among the most respected and effective militaries in the world, it is hampered by other challenges, such as ensuring that orthodox soldiers do not impermissibly encounter women. However understandable these accommodations are, no one suggests that they enhance readiness. I say this without shred of personal animus, but it is likewise impossible to suggest that gays in the U.S. military improve its ability to win wars, and that's all we need to know.

Women should be allowed in combat.

The logic of the previous section applies here as well, but there are some key distinctions. Women are of enormous value in today's military, often in capacities that require considerable strength and stamina. There are some who are surely of potential value in combat units. Yet this does not make their inclusion a good idea.

This will inflame all who look on the military as just another workplace. Employment discrimination is an obvious concern in the civilian world, but such concerns must be shelved in the military to achieve a fighting force with the greatest likelihood of survival and success. The rigors of war involve the necessary sacrifice of large portions of personal freedom, identity, and privacy, matters made even more complex when the close quarters of battle become coed.

The argument is not limited to physical capacity. It is possible that a sliver of the strongest, toughest women in a given Ranger class may edge out the bottom sliver of qualified men. But the chemistry of a war effort is far more complex.

Men and women are different, and men act differently around men than they do around women. The women willing and able to perform the tasks of combat will insist (and nobly so) that they're not looking for chivalry or special consideration. But it's not their choice. You can't turn off instinct like a light switch. The immutable wiring of men makes the mere presence of even the most battle-hardened woman in the trenches a distraction we cannot afford.

In a brilliant column in *War on the Rocks* titled "What Tempers the Steel of an Infantry Unit," retired Marine Lieutenant General Gregory Newbold sets aside all the irrelevant comparisons of physical characteristics and focuses on the fundamental reason why women in combat will never work. It is not about the talents, will, or patriotism of any woman; it is about a subject many seek to chase from our midst—the nature of manhood:

> The characteristics that produce uncommon valor as a common virtue are not physical at all, but are derived from the mysterious chemistry that forms in an infantry unit that revels in the most crude and profane existence so that they may be more effective killers than their foe. Members of such units deliberately reduce the individual and collective level of humanity and avoid all distractions so that its actions are fundamental, instinctive, and coldly efficient. Polite company, private hygiene, and weakness all step aside. These are the men who can confront the Islamic State, North Korean automatons, or Putin's Spetsnaz and win every time.[3]

I can hear platoons of women saying we don't care, send us in, we can handle it. And many probably can. But the men cannot, and they should not be asked to.

A Vietnam veteran told me of a conversation he had with comrades on the subject soon after their return, when the fires of feminism burned brightly, seeking "equality" even in areas where it was not germane. He told me the worst stories he was hearing were not of fellow soldiers tortured in prisoner of war camps; it was the stories of POWs who had to hear the anguished cries of their friends as *they* were tortured. They knew it was their job not to buckle under such brutality. But he told me he did not know if that directive would hold up amid the sounds of a woman POW having unspeakable things done to her down the hall.

"It's just too much to ask," he said, and he is right.

Women are not excluded from combat because they are unworthy or unwilling. Combat must remain men-only (and straight-men-only, at that) for one very clear reason: that is the fighting force that is most capable of winning wars. Nothing matters more.

22

THE SUPREME COURT

The court should be ideologically balanced.

America's political pendulum swings back and forth, reflecting changes in public opinion. This is exactly as it should be in a representative republic, where the leadership reflects what the people believe and thus how they vote.

But the Supreme Court is different. Its decisions should be based on the text of the U.S. Constitution. Not on fads and passions. Not on the justices' personal views. Not on the prevailing political winds. Not on prognostications of how a ruling might affect certain populations.

The model of judicial fidelity to the Constitution is the late Justice Antonin Scalia. In his personal views he was a conservative, but as a judge he was a constitutionalist—or as he would have put it, a "textualist"—which is the only thing that matters. Scalia did not try to defend or advance his personal views in his judicial opinions. He voted to uphold the First Amendment's protection of political expression he found abhorrent, like flag burning (*Texas v. Johnson*, 1989). In his dissent in *Obergefell v. Hodges* (2015), which imposed same-sex marriage on every state, he wrote, "The substance of today's decree is not of immense personal importance to me.... It is of overwhelming importance, however, who it is that rules me. Today's decree says that my Ruler, and the Ruler of 320 million Americans coast-to-coast, is a majority of the nine lawyers on the Supreme Court."

Scalia knew that the Constitution leaves marriage law to the states. Those that so desired could recognize gay unions as marriages, and those that did not could leave the institution as it was. But for the Left, the Supreme Court has become the legislature of last resort, where five sympathetic justices can enact laws that the Democrats couldn't get through Congress.

Judicial activism has been so successful that the Left is no longer coy about it. When President Obama introduced his nominee to replace Scalia, Merrick Garland, he touted the judge's creative credentials: "His life experience...informs his view that the law is more than an intellectual exercise. He understands the way law affects the daily reality of people's lives in a big, complicated democracy and in rapidly changing times."[1]

Fewer than forty words, and five large errors.

First, a judge's "life experience" should not "inform" his decisions. Education and constitutional fidelity, yes. Biography, no.

Second, the law *is* in fact an intellectual exercise, and it begins to unravel when it is twisted into something else. Textualist jurists use their intellect to cut through the fog of their own interests, preferences, and preoccupations in arriving at their judgments. That's what we used to call "the rule of law."

Third, "the way the law affects the daily reality of people's lives" is a matter for those who write laws, not those who judge their constitutionality. Every law benefits some and hinders others, and it's up to our elected representatives to sort that out. Allowing personal sympathies to shape Supreme Court rulings is the first step toward judicial tyranny.

Fourth, while democracy, like most of the cases that come before the Court, is complicated, that complexity should not obscure the singular simplicity of the Supreme Court's job—judging whether laws pass constitutional muster.

And fifth, whether the times are "rapidly changing" (when are they not?) is irrelevant. The passage of time and shifts in American values do not affect the necessity of squaring laws with the Constitution. If that eighteenth-century template proves inadequate to the exigencies of our time (as happens, though remarkably rarely), the Framers gave us the means of amending it. A vote of five Supreme Court justices, by the way, is not one of them.

What does it even mean for the Court to be ideologically "diverse"? That there are both conservatives and liberals on the bench? Fine. But if the liberals are unable to keep their political preferences out of their rulings, our system of law is in jeopardy. Judge Garland was praised as a "moderate," as if moderation in his adherence to constitutional principles were a virtue. Should he follow the Constitution only some of the time?

The proper arena for politics is Congress, where every interest can find its voice. But if a law enacted by Congress comes before the Supreme Court for a judgment on its compatibility with the Constitution, the megaphone of politics should give way to the blindfold of justice.

Supreme Court decisions make settled law.

"Settled law." It sounds so, well, *settled*.

The term is often affixed to a Supreme Court ruling the moment it is handed down. "Well, that's settled," say the factions satisfied with the result, amid the grumbling of those who are not.

Roe v. Wade has been "settled" for more than forty years now, but it settled nothing. Millions of Americans know abortion is mentioned nowhere in the text of the Constitution, and they will fight until the day of their own deaths to prevent as many deaths as they can from this contrived federal right.

Millions also know the Supreme Court erred in refusing to strike down Obamacare for its requirement that citizens engage in commerce they may not wish to pursue. Similarly, millions know that the court acted on a political rather than a constitutional basis in fabricating a right to gay marriage.

Anyone who thinks these issues are "settled" will learn otherwise if we are blessed with an infusion of originalist justices in the coming years. Those decisions will be overturned not because the court will have changed sides politically, but because it will have returned to its proper task of applying the Constitution as written.

So could that happen? Should it? It will be hard. Generations have grown up with legal and easily obtainable abortion, and the deadly logic of *Roe v. Wade* is now so deeply rooted that many pro-lifers despair of its ever being overturned. The Supreme Court encouraged that view when it reaffirmed *Roe* in *Planned Parenthood v. Casey* (1992), noting that "for two decades of economic and social developments, people have organized intimate relationships and made choices that define their views of themselves and their places in society, in reliance on the availability of abortion in the event that contraception should fail." The organization of "intimate relationships" has nothing to do with constitutional logic, but nonetheless, those two decades have stretched to four and half, further dimming the near-term hope of a correction.

The Obamacare and gay marriage decisions are far fresher, but defeatism has already sprouted among those who wonder if some future court can ever set things right.

Of course it can.

The main obstacle will be the legal principle of *stare decisis*, a deference to precedent that provides the predictability essential to the rule of law. Nevertheless, our written Constitution is the fundamental law of the land, and *stare decisis* cannot save a decision that seriously misconstrues it. If it could, we would still be living with Jim Crow.

But even if those constitutionally aberrant decisions are overturned, the rulings that replace them won't necessarily be "settled" either. Future justices may well renew the old abuses of a Constitution that is widely deemed to be at their mercy. This back-and-forth may ultimately affirm Solomon's observations about man's exploits: "all is vanity and a striving after wind."

Any nominee to the Supreme Court must be given a full hearing.

I felt sorry for Merrick Garland as his nomination to the Supreme Court was announced in March 2016. There in the Rose Garden stood a decent and admired man, bathed in the admiration of family and friends, on an occasion destined to lead precisely nowhere.

Invoking a precedent established by Democrats when presented with nominations late in the term of a Republican president, the leaders of the Senate had announced they had no intention of holding a vote on Garland before Barack Obama left office. Was this an affront to the Constitution or a call that GOP senators were free to make? The answer to that question is usually dictated by one's political preferences. Anyone hoping for a worthy successor to Antonin Scalia would have to hold out until a new Republican president could make the choice. For those eager for an unencumbered liberal majority on the Court, denying Obama his pick was an outrage. Who was right?

The Constitution identifies the Senate's role of "advice and consent" attendant to presidential nominations but stipulates no timetable. The Senate may fast-track nominations, slow-walk them, or express its disapproval by refusing to take them up at all. Senators can exercise a check on the president's ability to shape the Court, but they must calculate the political consequences of perceived obstructionism.

It was amusing to read editorials clearly stoking Obama's pick as they warned the Republicans who dared to stand in the way of this exit-ramp choice. Be careful, you crazy Republicans, came the warnings—you risk damaging your party if you don't allow hearings for Obama's nominee.

Apart from the feigned concern over the health of the GOP, those writers ignored the fact that blocking a late Obama Supreme Court pick was one of the most popular things the GOP Senate had done in years, a rare show of spine after a series of capitulations to the Obama agenda.

But the question fairly arose: how late is too late? Democrats pointed to Anthony Kennedy, confirmed in Ronald Reagan's final year of 1988. But that was for a vacancy created by the retirement of Lewis Powell in June 1987. The intervening spectacle was the savaging of Robert Bork, nominated in July but unjustly rejected in October. Then came the fleeting nomination of Douglas Ginsburg, whose nomination vanished in the blue smoke of his admitted marijuana usage as recently as the decade before. So that's why the Kennedy vote took place in Reagan's final year.

If Scalia had passed away in June 2015, there would have been no argument for denying a hearing for an Obama nominee. But with the presidential primary season already under way and nominating conventions just five months down the road, there was a strong case for giving voters a more direct say in the nomination. Let the Supreme Court appointment be an issue in the presidential election, said the advocates of a delay, many admittedly because they did not want to see Obama fill the Scalia seat with a justice far less devoted to the Constitution.

May I suggest an admittedly arbitrary but usefully bright line for situations like this? If a Supreme Court vacancy occurs before January 1 of a presidential election year, the Senate should give full consideration to a nominee. If the vacancy occurs on or after January 1, the seat should be held open for the next president to fill. That would be a small but important step to restoring good will and efficiency to a process that needs both.

23

THE OBAMA ERA

Obama is the most hated president ever.

A little surfing of the cable channels these days can turn up some unflattering takes on the Obama presidency. You might even catch the occasional lament that this is the worst presidency ever. But is Barack Obama the most *hated* president ever? His supporters, demanding sympathy, want you to think so.

Martin Van Buren would probably disagree. When he sought reelection in 1840, his opponents expressed their views in a popular song:

Who never did a noble deed
Who of the people took no heed
Who is the worst of tyrant's breed—Van Buren!

It gets better:

Who rules us with an iron rod
Who heeds not man, who heeds not God
Who moves at Satan's beck and rod—Van Buren!

And the big finish:

Who would his friends his country sell
Do other deeds too base to tell
Deserves the lowest place in Hell—Van Buren!

Van Buren lost that election.

It's tricky, of course, to compare political invective from different eras. But I don't recall any sound bites from a Fox News roundtable saying Obama "moves at Satan's beck and rod," and I haven't heard Rush Limbaugh wrap up a segment with the suggestion that he "deserves the lowest place in Hell...let's go to your calls."

Does anyone remember Richard Nixon? Bill Clinton? Lyndon Johnson endured the taunting chant "Hey, hey, LBJ, how many kids did you kill today?" Democrats dubbed the squalid shantytowns of the Great Depression "Hoovervilles," a cruel jab at a deeply compassionate man who during World War I had almost single-handedly saved millions of people from starvation.

It's easy to forget that some of our most admired presidents were also the most hated. Before the Left extended a few grudging gestures of civility when he died in 2004, Ronald Reagan was despised as a reckless, half-witted cowboy, an "amiable dunce" with the nuclear codes. And of course Abraham Lincoln, now enthroned in a marble temple on the National Mall, was reviled in his lifetime by half the country. There is still a bar in North Carolina, where the bottoms of the urinals feature a penny, face up.

Post-presidential goodwill can sometimes erase memories of the grilling some of our chief executives received while in office. Jimmy Carter, who proved more inspiring as a Habitat for Humanity home-builder than as commander in chief, is frequently praised as one of our greatest ex-presidents. Who remembers the Iranian hostage crisis or an 18 percent prime interest rate?

Carter was the first presidential candidate I ever voted against. Three years into his one and only term of office, he addressed the American people about a "crisis of confidence that strikes at the very heart and soul and spirit of our national will," evident in "the grow-ing doubt about the meaning of our own lives and in the loss of a unity of purpose for our nation."[1] I joined millions in weariness but never doubted the meaning of my own life, and the following year forty-four million of us recovered our unity of purpose and returned Jimmy Carter to private life. Thirty years later his presidency was still a byword for failure, inspiring a T-shirt featuring Barack Obama's image accompanied by flowery 1970s lettering and a TV reference: "Welcome Back, Carter."

Recent presidents may seem more despised because of the twenty-four-hour news cycle. Obama faces an unrelenting stream of attacks that was unknown to Franklin Pierce, for example. But if cable tele-vision had been around to cover the presidencies of the polarizing Pierce, John Tyler (kicked out of his own party), Millard Fillmore (generally viewed as inert), James Buchanan (embroiled in pre-Civil War invective), and Andrew Johnson (impeached and one vote shy of ejection from office), Obama's rough ride might not have seemed so bad.

In fact, Obama enjoys an advantage that none of these previous punching-bag presidents had: a large chorus of defenders suggesting that his critics are bigots (see next section). Critics finding fault with Obama's policies (which are the fuel of 99 percent of the unflatter-ing things said about him) will find their motives impugned, the implication being that their real problem with Obama is his race. Sadly, plenty of people believe this nonsense.

Conservatives hate Obama because he is black.

President Obama's is hardly the only voice saying race motivates his opponents. Long before he became comfortable insulting his critics as racists, many of his allies did it for him, even before he took office.

During the 2008 campaign, as it became clear that Obama would edge out Hillary Clinton for the Democratic nomination, liberals began to anticipate the ads and opinion pieces that he would face during the general election campaign. The kind of opposition that would have been raised against any Democratic nominee, they recognized, could now be parried as racist.

After he became president, Obama produced a target-rich environment for his opponents—an economically ruinous stimulus that stimulated nothing, a health care plan that raised costs and invaded the doctor-patient relationship, and a retreat from the war against terrorists, to name but a few. Yet every criticism of the Messiah President could be deflected as antipathy to his blackness. Why waste your breath defending his policies when you can shut down a debate in seconds by marginalizing your opponent as a hater?

So let's put this to the test. Do conservatives loathe black people?

In March 2016, there was anxiety about an open national convention that might overturn the preference of Republican voters for an insurgent candidate, Donald Trump and Ted Cruz having captured roughly 80 percent of the delegates to that point. Most fears were focused on an attempt to force-feed an establishment darling, such as the thoroughly defeated Jeb Bush, or either half of the Mitt

Romney-Paul Ryan ticket that lost a winnable election in 2012. Speaking to a conservative audience that month, I asked if there was anyone the party could draft who would excite them. The first three waves of enthusiasm were for former Secretary of State Condoleezza Rice and former Congressmen Allen West and J. C. Watts. Anything strike you about that trio?

Race matters less as time passes, and that is a wonderful thing. Beliefs shape our tastes these days, which is why most blacks love Bill Clinton and have no use for Clarence Thomas. It is why a crowd of conservative white folks will give Ben Carson standing ovations while turning a cold shoulder to Chuck Schumer.

This is no less true of Barack Obama. If criticism of him seems particularly harsh at times, it is because his agenda has been radical and polarizing. By making it clear that he regards his political opponents as enemies to be vanquished, he has fed their fear that everything they hold dear is at stake. No one can be surprised that civility does not thrive in such an environment.

Obama has improved race relations.

The first African-American presidency should have been a watershed in race relations. The ebb of racism made the Obama presidency possible. Irrespective of politics, the election of our first black president was an occasion to celebrate real diversity embraced by real people at the ballot box.

What a shame that occasion was squandered.

The first black president should have proclaimed in all he said and did, "I am living proof of the greatness of our nation and its capacity for progress. I want to be a force for expanding harmony between all races. I am evidence that Dr. King's dream of an America in which we are judged not by the color of our skin but by the content of our character is alive."

Maybe the next president of color can say that. This one won't. Throughout his two terms he has stoked racial antagonism at every opportunity.

At this point in our history, disturbances in race relations are not the result of residual bigotry; they are the work of political opportunists following Obama's lead, never missing an opportunity to broaden racial divides.

George Zimmerman's shooting of Trayvon Martin, the shooting of Michael Brown by a cop in Ferguson, Missouri, the arrest of Harvard professor Henry Louis Gates—all of these afforded the president a chance to calm the public with a reasoned call to assess the facts as they became available. He had no interest in such measured rationality, preferring to exacerbate tensions for political gain.

The Obama administration is not alone in fueling racial resentment. Democrats at every level continue to peddle the lie of white oppression, in effect telling blacks that they dare not rely on their own gifts in the free markets of a free country. They must support a massive welfare state, maintain racial preferences in hiring and education, and keep a lookout for racist conservatives who are eager, as Vice President Biden tactfully put it, to "put y'all back in chains."

No wonder people think race relations are backsliding. The president and the media are constantly poking the race beehive. Repeated outbursts over racial matters can disguise the broader truth that racism is fading with every passing generation. When George W. Bush left office, 76 percent of blacks felt blacks and whites got along "very well" or "pretty well." By Obama's second term, that figure had dropped 12 points.[2] Obama cares about black people, all right—he cares about making sure they doubt America's racial progress and the growing goodwill that drives real racism deeper into society's dank-est corners.

Every American should have wished for Obama to succeed.

Before Rush Limbaugh got the "Do you want the new president to succeed" question in 2009, I had fielded it in 1993. On the morning of Bill Clinton's inauguration, I was hosting my local Washington morning show from a hotel on Capitol Hill, affording me the chance to walk a few blocks to see the installation of the second successful presidential candidate I had not voted for.

"Don't you want President Clinton to succeed?" someone asked me. I knew his success would mean the enactment of various policies I deeply disagreed with, but it just seemed so snarky to say no. So I said something like, "Well, yes, in the sense that I want any president to succeed because he's a president for all the people, and we should all want some level of success for any new president. But in a way no, because if he succeeds at doing certain things, it might mean the country is not in fact succeeding, which means we have to determine what we want success for, a president or the nation.... " Yikes. After that Mr. Bojangles tap-dance, I slept on the question and determined that it deserved a direct and better-crafted answer. So the next morning I came back with one.

"Imagine your child is sick," I told whatever remained of the audience. "A doctor is on the way, but when you open the door, it is a witch doctor ready to work on your child with a number of scary treatments, some of which may not work and some of which actually seem harmful." Metaphor successfully deployed, I offered the bottom line: "Do you want the witch doctor to succeed?"

I had shown that the question was based on a false premise. What we want is a proper doctor to administer effective treatments. In my example, that would be the definition of success; a child made healthier because of the right treatment. The witch doctor's "succeeding" was a non sequitur because no definition of success included the things he was likely to do.

I decided not to deploy the witch doctor metaphor for the Obama inauguration sixteen years later, but nonetheless found a way to answer the same question with clarity. No, I did not want Obama to succeed, because his policy successes would bring about results antithetical to my wishes for the country.

I stand vindicated.

Obamacare passed. Trillions squandered in an ever-expanding government. Gay marriage forced on unwilling states. Withdrawal from the war against terror. By any measure, the Obama agenda has succeeded, leading to precisely what I feared in 2009—his successes accumulating to the actual detriment of the nation.

24

CONSERVATISM

Conservatives are anti-government.

The next time a crew of extremists commit some irrational or violent act against their perceived government tormentors, count the seconds until someone tries to connect them with mainstream conservatism.

Dick Morris, a former advisor to Bill Clinton who has since changed his political stripes, came up with talking points for the White House in 1995 blaming conservative talk radio for the Oklahoma City bombing. Democrats and the media routinely suggest that conservative voices have incited one misdeed or another. The evidence? Conservatives are "anti-government."

The Southern Poverty Law Center, which specializes in slandering conservative organizations as "hate groups," cited the 2015 standoff with armed occupiers of a federal wildlife refuge in Oregon as evidence of a surge in "anti-government" passions, encouraging the public to equate ordinary citizens who are dismayed by the growth of government with violent kooks.[1]

Some of the groups the SPLC identifies as extremists are in fact extremists, but it also impugns groups who identify as "patriots" or profess deep fidelity to the Constitution, as if those views are a sign of hatred of the government. Conservatives of every stripe want less government than we have now. The desire to return to the strong but limited government designed by our nation's architects does not make you anti-government; it makes you anti-*huge*-government. Conservatives oppose government tyranny, overreach, bloat, waste, expansionism, collectivism, and intrusiveness, resisting the belief that government can solve every problem.

When a budget impasse between Congressional Republicans and President Obama threatened a shutdown of the federal government in 2013, liberals shouted, "See? We told you they hated government!" Conservatives welcomed the opportunity to prove that big portions of government could close and the earth would somehow continue to turn. As the deadline approached, cries went up that a government shutdown would bring unbearable pain to the nation and inflict irreparable political damage on the Republicans.

After the sixteen-day shutdown—"slowdown" would be more accurate—life snapped back to normal for virtually everyone. And the next time voters had a chance to show Republicans what they thought of them, they awarded them a Senate majority and their largest House majority since 1928. Electoral results at the state level were an equally emphatic high-five for the GOP.[2]

Conservatives show justifiable disdain for what our government has become. It takes too much of our money, it spends it improperly, it pokes its nose into our private business, it too often curbs rather than protects our liberties. Restoring the government to its proper constitutional proportions is not an attack; it's rehabilitation. Taming the modern federal leviathan is not a show of scorn for the noble enterprise of self-government; it is the restoration of the most admirable design for such government that man has yet devised.

Conservative tax reforms coddle the rich.

The fact that the wealthy pay too much in taxes—way too much—is one of the toughest truths to sell on the campaign trail. Most conservatives don't even try.

Why are we embarrassed to oppose the punishment of success? Some Republicans have summoned enough courage to advocate a flat tax, but what is that if not a relief for upper-level earners from the confiscatory rates they currently pay?

The *Wall Street Journal* prepped its readers for Tax Day 2015 with a look at who pays what. The top 20 percent of earners—a group that starts at about $135,000 a year—make about half of the total income earned in the United States, but they pay 84 percent of the total taxes. Federal income taxes don't begin to bite until we make about fifty thousand dollars.[3] PR advisers warn conservatives not to talk about "makers and takers," but what other conclusion is there?

People at the highest income levels usually get there by doing something that earns a financial reward, such as starting a business, making things, and employing people. Imagine if such people were treated more equitably when it came time for the government to exact its pound of flesh. People in a free economy are driven by the profit motive, which is nothing to apologize for. Businesses earn more money by making and doing more things, allowing them to expand and hire and, as a result, pay more taxes. The way to fill the national treasury is not to rob people as their earnings increase but to allow them to keep more of what they earn so that their money can circulate several times through the economy, to everyone's benefit.

A favorite Democratic taunt is "tax cuts for the rich." But a flat tax, which would indeed be a tax cut for the rich, is not only what our economy needs, it is the definition of fair. The obstacle to this worthy policy is the continuing appeal of free stuff paid for by other people.

A truth is no less true for being hard to sell. Conservatives seeking tax relief for upper earners are not greedy; they are attempting to restore fairness and common sense to a system that currently tells the most productive members of society to work, earn, and spend less.

Conservatives are blind to the stigma of slavery.

There's a familiar American conversational pattern that has taken on the rhythm of an endless tape loop. Someone states a current racial grievance. His interlocutors may agree or disagree with the validity of the grievance, but eventually the person who originally brought it up will remind everyone that slavery happened.

And we're done.

Anyone questioning the relevance of slavery, 150 years after its abolition, to twenty-first-century problems, is accused of insensitivity to its lingering (eternal?) stigma. Here's a thoughtful path forward when someone throws the conversation-ending slavery punch.

First, no one should ever suggest that black Americans should "get over" slavery. I cannot imagine what it is like to live with the legacy of my ancestors' having suffered under the whip. One may suggest that the horrors of slavery are not relevant to one modern issue or another, but no one whose forebears were dragged to this nation in chains can ever just put that on a forgotten shelf.

Beyond that, it is useful to observe that though the historical pace of racial healing has in general been agonizingly slow, there have been bursts of rapid progress. A hundred years after slavery ended, whites-only water fountains could still be found across the South. But less than a decade after the Civil Rights Act of 1964, racism was considered one of the darkest perspectives a person could harbor. A nation afflicted with deep racial wounds has healed them through legislation and goodwill.

Racism still exists, but it has been driven deep into the caves of unacceptable utterance. Our racial progress has been nothing short of a social miracle, especially the fast track of the last fifty years. Yet it is suggested that the problems of black America are still largely the result of slavery. If this were 1890, 1920, even 1950, that argument might hold water. It was a long road from the Emancipation Proclamation to real racial enlightenment. But it is here. It has the force of law, and every level of decent society participates in it.

The most extreme version of the slavery-is-still-to-blame argument calls for reparations—actual monetary reimbursement—for the bondage of past centuries. As recently as 2014, Congressman John Conyers of Michigan called for a commission to study the possibilities. But how would that work? Who would pay? Who would receive? No living American of any race had anything to do with slavery, yet every taxpayer would be on the hook. And would every black American get a check? What about the many black Americans—like President Obama—who are not the descendants of slaves? Would there be means-testing, or would Oprah Winfrey and Tyler Perry get their slice? Are all blacks, rich and poor and middle-class, equally wounded by slavery? Or are their fortunes, like everyone else's, the results of their life choices, work ethic, dumb luck?

To dismiss reparations as a ridiculous fantasy is not to dismiss the residual harm of slavery. Americans of every other color should appreciate that their black countrymen are the only ones who are here because their progenitors were enslaved on this soil.

That said, I had an unforgettable call one day in the 1990s from a black listener to my radio show in Washington. A young professional, he told me about a conversation he had with some upwardly mobile black friends. "We were talking about slavery," he said, "and we obviously deplore the concept. But then someone mentioned that without it I probably wouldn't be raising my kids in America in a nice house in Bethesda." I asked the caller how he, or anyone, responds to that irony of history. "You just compartmentalize," he said. "I am grateful every day to be in America. That doesn't mean I have to celebrate how my great-great-great-great grandparents got here."

I don't suggest that my black readers, listeners, and friends should reevaluate the horrors of slavery because of where the road eventually led. But I do suggest that context is vital. The practice of slavery was common around the world; America was not uniquely wicked in maintaining it. But America was unique in fighting a Civil War to end it. Indeed, Abraham Lincoln suggested that that war itself might have been a kind of reparation:

> The Almighty has His own purposes. "Woe unto the world because of offenses; for it must needs be that offenses come, but woe to that man by whom the offense cometh." If we shall suppose that American slavery is one of those offenses which, in the providence of God, must needs come, but which, having continued through His appointed time, He now wills to remove, and that He gives to both North and South this terrible war as the woe due to those by whom

the offense came, shall we discern therein any departure from those divine attributes which the believers in a living God always ascribe to Him?

Might we also suggest that reparations have been paid through decades of affirmative action? It is hard to imagine a more targeted atonement than policies that accrued specifically to the advantage of the descendants of slaves.

None of these arguments suggests insensitivity to the moral stain of slavery. But it is possible to appreciate its history while resisting its exhumation as a modern political weapon.

Conservatives are eager for war.

In 1991, I served as MC for a rally in Washington, filmed by C-SPAN, supporting Operation Desert Storm, which was well on the way to kicking Saddam Hussein's forces out of Kuwait. When the event was broadcast, the title at the bottom of the screen read "Pro-Administration War Rally."[4]

C-SPAN is a national treasure, but that bugged me. The rally was not primarily about our support for the administration and was certainly not a broad celebration of war. It was about the need for military action to thwart a global evil. We have faced a few of those, and we have responded—not because we are a warlike people, but because we have chosen not to let evil prevail without a response.

More than twenty-five years later, the war with radical Islamists still raging, those of us who would very much like to defeat them are pilloried as bloodthirsty warmongers. American public opinion has seen multiple shifts since 9/11. For a while, we were nearly united in the cause of crushing the regimes that wanted to harm us, most prominently Iraq. When we didn't wrap that up quickly, the Left hunkered into a familiar stance: revulsion at the notion of the American military as a force for good, intensified by hatred for President George W. Bush.

Just a few years into the war, things were not going well. Deep into the second Bush term, even some war supporters had grown weary. It was a hard time to suggest that what was needed was a serious ramp-up of the war effort, but then, as now, there is a basic truth of war—that there is but one way to win, and that is to kill enough of the enemy that it decides to stop fighting you.

That is why we won World Wars I and II and the first Gulf War, why we did not win in Korea, and why we lost so dreadfully in Vietnam. This is another bitter truth that conservatives must deliver, that war is sometimes necessary and always hard.

Conservatives are called war-hungry because we advocate a strong military. This is not so that we can use it; it is so that we do not have to. Ronald Reagan famously said that no war in his lifetime came about because America was too strong. American weakness, however, invites dangers that push us toward war's cliffsides.

The reluctance and weakness of the Obama administration has plopped us into a stew featuring multiple threats of war. Iran is feeling adventurous, ISIS is on the march worldwide, and North Korea toys with us on a regular basis. These situations will not instantly improve when a strong president takes office, but a resolute leader backed by a restored military will send a message around the world that we are no longer to be trifled with. War will then be less likely.

Leftists say peace is impossible if we're preparing for war. In fact, that's the *only* way to improve the chances of peace—when tyrants and terrorists know we are ready to meet their threat.

Conservatives want to take America backward.

The Left likes to whine that Republicans want to "turn back the clock." People who talk that way usually have abortion in mind. The funny thing is, conservatives actually *are* trying to return to pre–*Roe v. Wade* America, but we consider this a step forward, toward a time of rediscovered sanctity for human life in all forms.

Conservatives want to recover the good things we have lost. We'd like to get back to schools where the common behavior problems are talking and dress code violations rather than stabbings and sexual assaults. We'd like out-of-wedlock births to be uncommon again. We'd like to teach kids that America is a virtuous nation to be cherished.

We'd like to retrieve the optimism that allowed children to believe their lives would be better than their parents' were. We'd like to return to a work ethic that celebrates the value of self-esteem resulting from actual achievement. We'd like to get back to spending levels that do not doom every man, woman, and child in America to crushing per capita debt. We'd like to get back to colleges that challenge students intellectually and form them morally in an atmosphere of genuine freedom without "safe zones" and "trigger warnings."

So yes, there are some things from the past that are missed, and not just by conservatives. But the smear is that we yearn for those good old days before women and minorities had all of these pesky rights. We would indeed like to return to a time when chivalry was not mocked and when cops were respected by all races. It is often said that not all progress is good. Sometimes it seems that very little of it is.

Plenty of competing ideas will duke it out as our nation's future unfolds. No one seeks to take us backward on actual rights or precious enlightenment. But progressives have driven us into some ditches. Conservatives do not wish to turn around to undo progress; we wish to combine the best of new ideas with a retooling of what some folks thought were good ideas but have not turned out to be.

25

LIBERALISM

Liberals care more about people.

One exit poll from the 2012 presidential election made Mitt Romney's loss particularly painful. Respondents were asked which attributes of the candidates drove their votes. Romney won among those looking for a candidate who "shares my values," "is a strong leader," and "has a vision for the future." But voters looking for someone who "cares about people like me" favored Obama by a margin of 81 to 18.[1]

Caring is a funny thing. I want a family that cares about me and a pastor who cares about me, and I love my dogs because they care about me. I don't care if the president cares about me. I want a president who can run the country while leaving me alone to look after myself.

Be very afraid when politicians start saying how much they care about people. Their caring usually involves taking a great deal of money from some and giving it to others. The recipients may get a warm cared-for feeling, but those paying the bill just feel burned.

Caring is a magnificent quality in real people. It takes the form of kindness, charity, and outreach, ennobling the person who gives of himself. Government, however, cannot "care." It has nothing to give except what it has taken from others, and its attempts at benevolence have not worked well. So how can government show it has our best interests at heart? By enacting only the laws needed for social order and the protection of our liberties. Then leave us to enjoy those liberties, guaranteeing greater freedom and prosperity for all.

Officials who show that kind of restraint, who respect our capacity for self-government, "care" about us far more than the redistributors do. But it is the liberals, perpetuating a culture of dependency, who get the credit for caring about us. Which is the more caring parent, the one who meets his children's basic needs and gives them the opportunity to flourish on their own or the one who lets them live in the basement until they're thirty?

That's not caring, it's enabling.

As with many issues, the initial battle is over language. The Left's definition of caring is based on a government model. Attempts to replace unwieldy government solutions with private-sector alternatives are condemned as heartless. In 2011, Congressman Paul Ryan's Medicare reform plan—a thoughtful attempt to save a program everyone cares about—provoked television ads depicting him shoving an elderly woman in a wheelchair off a cliff.

Subtlety is not on the menu when liberals attack conservative solutions. Rather than argue the superior merits of their ideas, they try to squelch debate by demonizing opponents as villains unworthy of a place in the debate. "We care about you, they don't" is a myth that has taken hold broadly.

Conservatives could do a better job of selling their ideas. Facts, figures, and history are useful tools, but they are sadly lost on many. Without abandoning the meat of their arguments, conservatives should display a desire to improve the lives of Americans in tangible ways, wrapping those ideas in parables that today's short attention spans can comprehend.

It might seem glib to say conservative approaches are more beneficial to the citizenry at large, while many liberal solutions are about expansion of government and the accrual of more money and power by politicians. But if one side is going to suggest that it cares more about you, isn't that a track record worth examining?

Has a caring Obama administration made life better for American workers? Has it encouraged self-worth by moving people off the welfare rolls? Has it brought health care costs down? Has it made us safer?

How is liberal caring working out in our big cities, almost always run by Democratic mayors? Are the schools well run? Is crime under control? Are the neighborhoods healthy and thriving?

Enough about who cares more. Instead of indulging liberals' pretentions to have cornered the market on virtue, let's insist on a clear-eyed assessment of the results.

Liberalism deserves praise for its good intentions.

The last line of defense for any of the policy disasters that liberals have inflicted on the United States—massive expansion of the government, coddling international bullies, an exploding welfare state,

Obamacare, business-crippling minimum wage targets, to name a few—is that "they meant well."

It is hard to imagine anything more irrelevant. Do good intentions make ideas better? The worst tyrants tell the oppressed that they have their best interests at heart, and some, in their twisted view, actually may.

I always say that the worst thing I want to accuse liberals of is being mistaken. Having bad ideas does not make one contemptible. There are indeed certain low tactics and accompanying behaviors that earn personal scorn—and that's true across the political spectrum—but we should strive to keep our disagreements ideological rather than personal.

Unfortunately, President Obama rarely misses an opportunity to characterize the motivations of his opponents in the darkest possible terms. Differ with him on economics, and you are cruel and greedy. Differ with him on the environment, and you are indifferent to the fate of the planet. Differ with him on LGBT issues, and you are a hateful bigot. Differ with him on almost anything, and you are probably a racist.

Obama's own intentions have been the subject of debate. Is he merely misguided, or is he ideologically committed to diminishing this nation? If a president wanted to endanger the economy and our security, he could scarcely do a more efficient job than enacting Obama's agenda.

I'll leave the mind-reading to others and give the president the benefit of the doubt, because his intentions make no difference. Bad ideas are bad ideas, even if offered sincerely. Those ideas can be criticized without savaging the people who hold them. But it is foolish to spare the criticism just because those people think they are looking out for us.

Liberalism benefits minorities and women.

It looks like a majority of women and minorities are in the Democrats' pocket and will be for a while. So what fuels that affinity? A cursory analysis suggests that women vote Democrat because they view the party as more touchy-feely, and minorities vote Democrat because they think that's the only party that likes them—an unflattering theory in which there is probably a nugget of truth. Republicans sound like scolds to many women, and they sound disapproving to many blacks and Hispanics. This probably leads back to the communication and packaging improvements the GOP needs to undertake immediately.

Conservatism would surely earn more female votes if it did not seek to constrain them from extinguishing their pregnancies. That's not going to change, so it must be made up for in other ways. In her 2012 book, *Ladies, Can We Talk?* my Dallas friend Debbie Georgatos warns, "Candidates target women with political messaging that is designed to subtly persuade us to abandon our reason and logic and be swept away by emotion."[2] She believes female voters' leftward tilt is counterintuitive: "Most women I know would not voluntarily embrace a controlling, domineering father, boyfriend or spouse.... But many of us have sat silently as government becomes more aggressive, intrusive, powerful, controlling and condescending."

I have heard the theory that women, who historically looked to their husbands for protection, now look to the government for that protection. I have no interest in putting that one under the microscope; in fact, all of these excuses for why women lean left seem empty. At the moment, they just do. Is this immovable?

Richard Nixon won the women's vote by 24 percentage points in his 1972 reelection. Ronald Reagan won them by two points in 1980, twelve in 1984. George H. W. Bush squeaked out a 50-to-49 margin among women in 1998, and his son George W. lost them by only three in 2004.[3] It's not as though women have permanently closed the door to Republicans, but that door needs to be opened by candidates who can remind women of the conservative roots of protecting our nation, affording equality of opportunity, and standing up for the social values which respect womanhood all the way back into the womb.

Minority voting is an even bigger target for such an effort. Few environments are as socially conservative as black churches; Hispanic culture celebrates family bonds and entrepreneurship. The first step to winning the votes of minorities is to sweep away the fallacy that the Republican Party doesn't want them.

Latino citizens should be the first to embrace the conservative goal of a strong border, protecting their livelihoods from incursions by illegal immigrants. Black voters should note that conservative circles celebrate African-American conservatism with a special passion.

Has Barack Obama, our first black president, brought black unemployment closer to the level of whites? Has he healed the racial divisions he described (if not exploited) to win in the first place? Has he welcomed voucher programs that would instantly give inner-city children a shot at a better education?

Democratic "solutions" to many problems can be downright hazardous to minority Americans. Hiking the minimum wage will price countless workers of color out of the job market; "sentencing reform" will release streams of offenders back into their communities.

Most issues affect men and women in the same way, with no great differences across racial lines. There is just no reason for the double-digit "gender gap" of the last two presidential elections or the nearly 80 percent gap between white and non-white Republican voting.

Black Republican vote totals in presidential elections have more than doubled from the 4 percent levels of the 1980s to the 10-to-12-percent range seen in the elections since 2000. As Lao Tzu said, a journey of a thousand miles begins with a single step. But the journey for conservatives is well worth making. It involves doing the work to earn minority votes, the first step of which is to sincerely ask for them.

As for women whose main obstacle to voting Republican remains "reproductive freedom," we should explain that we are not coming for their birth control pills and stress that even if we do get *Roe v. Wade* overturned, it won't mean an abortion ban, just the ability of states to craft their own abortion laws, as restrictively or as leniently as voters wish.

In short, the conservative task is to dispel a host of misconceptions. In fairness, some GOP candidates haven't helped, committing unforced errors that perpetuate those misconceptions. This is the time for a charm offensive, an effort that combines bold truths with a pleasant countenance. They are not mutually exclusive, and they could go a long way toward disabusing millions of minorities and women of the notion that their fates are umbilically linked to liberal politics.

Liberals love America just as much as conservatives do.

This one needs a qualifier: many do. I have liberal friends whose love for America I would equate with my own. Others, not so much.

Here's the difference. What kind of liberal do we mean? If liberals and conservatives love America equally but simply envision different paths to improvement, that's fine. And that probably accounts for the majority of Americans.

But much of today's leftist thought involves denigration of America's motives, its influence, its national character. President Obama isn't the only Democratic politician to express such views, but he's a useful place to start.

Does one love a country that needs to be apologized for around the world? Does one love a country that is to blame for tensions in the Middle East? Does one love a country filled with racists and

Islamophobes? Does one love a country where the police are predators? Does one love a country that needs to be "fundamentally changed?" Does one show love for America by befriending its harshest critics? Does one love a nation whose founders were just old misguided white men?

These criticisms ring through the rhetoric of the Left. They say they love America, but they surely do not admire it very much—not its origins, not its Constitution. For others on the Left, there is love for what they want to turn America into, but not for the nation as it is. To them, only when we have humbled ourselves before a disapproving world, only when we have dropped our annoying concern about who crosses our borders, only when we have scolded Israel for being as evil as Hamas and Hezbollah, only when we have strangled our businesses with a fifteen-dollar minimum wage, only when we have shaken down our wealthy to distribute their earnings on others, only when we have shredded and rewritten our Constitution to reflect modern progressive ideals—only then will we be a nation worthy of respect.

26

LIBERTARIANISM

The American military should not be used as a force for good around the world.

Our libertarian brothers and sisters, who are so right on so many issues involving the size, scope, and cost of government, nevertheless would limit the American government in the one area where it has contributed most to the world and may be needed most urgently in the years to come.

In the century since America entered World War I, the U.S. armed forces have compiled an unparalleled track record of freeing people from tyranny, beating back expansionist despots, and spreading democracy and self-determination. This success does not mean that every world trouble spot requires American intervention, but it does demand a careful re-evaluation by those who would restrict our international influence.

Libertarians share a commitment to limited government with the nation's Founders, who drew up a Constitution painstakingly enumerating the powers granted to the three federal branches. Our misadventures beyond that framework have landed us in our current fiscal mess. But while we're looking for ways to save money, there is great hazard in gutting the American military and its ability to contribute to a stable world.

Libertarians are not pacifists. If an enemy strikes our shores they are ready to respond, but usually only as far as erecting some fortress to fend off further attacks. The concept of taking a war to the part of the world where the attacks originated offends their otherwise admirable devotion to smaller government.

Wars are tremendously expensive, but military ventures cannot be judged by financial cost alone. What do we get in return? Few argue that our victories in two world wars weren't worth it, but thereafter the cost-benefit analysis gets complicated. What did our involvement in Korea achieve? By any measure, we lost in Vietnam. And after more than a decade of war against terrorists, opponents of the war can rightfully say we have fallen short.

But is insufficient engagement an argument against war in the first place? Perhaps our failure to contain terrorists indicates not the folly of trying but the inadequacy of our strategy? Ramping up the U.S. war effort in the Middle East with large new troop deployments would send libertarians into convulsions. They see big war efforts as more big government, subject to the same dangers of corruption and bloat as every other kind of government program.

The libertarian heroine Ayn Rand, driven by her opposition to communism, was more hawkish than her post–Cold War disciples. Her example should be a beacon for the true friends of liberty. Those forces that would crush freedoms around the world cannot be allowed to succeed.

Our nation's Founders knew well the arrogance of colonialism. Our revolution has inspired nations large and small whose people dream of the freedoms we take for granted. A strong and involved America can free entire populations from oppression. We do so not because we seek to colonize or subjugate others, but because we know the spread of liberty around the world is conducive to peace and stability and thus to our own security.

It is popular to say we cannot be the world's policeman, and that would be true if a police force had to respond to everything. But without a vigilant and powerful America, global trouble spots could well get worse, ultimately increasing the threat to our domestic freedoms that libertarians spend their lives protecting.

People should be free to use drugs until they commit a crime.

If isolationism doesn't hinder the appeal of libertarianism, there's always that pesky urge to legalize drugs. Moved by an admirable desire to let people do what they wish in their own lives, libertarians lose sight of the obvious fact that an intoxicated society is everyone's business.

While my life is not directly harmed if my neighbor is smoking, shooting, dropping, or snorting his preferred toxins, what about when he gets behind the wheel? What if his impaired state leads him to do something crazy and destructive? What if the drug habits of huge numbers of Americans affect our national work ethic, our morals, our family integrity?

Alcohol presents the same problems, of course, and we have shown we do not have the national desire to outlaw it. But just because one widely consumed intoxicant is ingrained in our society, do we have to introduce others? Is our society better off with more intoxicants available? The pro-legalization side would like you to think so. They call our current policy "drug prohibition" to associate it with the failed attempt to ban alcohol in the 1920s and '30s. The difference is that the consumption of alcohol has been part of our culture since the dawn of recorded history. The other dalliances we have concocted or discovered are another matter entirely, with usage reduced by the laws that attach penalties to possession and consumption.

So what's the problem with allowing the possession and consumption of drugs, imposing penalties only when users harm others? It is crushingly myopic. Are we to wait for the stoned driver to kill my kids? For the tweaked-out addict to commit some heinous offense? No, thanks. Far better to stem the behavior that contributes to the offense in the first place.

Sometimes freedoms conflict and have to be balanced. We should be free to do what we wish on our own time with our own money in our own lives without government interference, but we should also be free to decide collectively what threats to society we will and will not permit.

America has become a police state.

Another laudable strand of libertarian thought is its devotion to privacy. The world is full of intrusive regimes that stick their noses into the business of citizens. In the debate over what law enforcement should and should not be able to do, some Americans are punctuating their arguments with comparisons to those repressive regimes.

The "police state" argument pops up in connection with two questions in particular: What are the police allowed to do, and how heavily armed should they be? The Fourth Amendment protects us from "unreasonable searches and seizures," but it doesn't define "unreasonable." We do not have warrantless midnight raids of homes, but Transportation Security Administration agents examine us with varying degrees of intimacy at the airport. "Stop and frisk" policies permit police to detain a person briefly under suspicious circumstances. "No refusal" DWI enforcement deprives motorists of the option to decline roadside blood alcohol tests.

Some Americans believe we have tipped the scales too far in favor of law enforcement. TSA screening can seem too tactile for some and a waste of time for others, but it can be avoided by not flying. DWI enforcement is not an experience that comes to our homes; it is part of the heavily regulated environment of our roads. "Stop and frisk" became controversial because of perceptions that the stopping and frisking was happening disproportionately to minorities. That's worth keeping an eye on, but it's also worth noting that minorities disproportionately occupy neighborhoods where frisking is most justified.

The ubiquitous cameras in our lives drive libertarians crazy. Some object to electronic eyes that capture activity along entire blocks; most object to the traffic signal cameras designed to keep us from running red lights. I love the cameras on the street that might help identify a suspect in an assault. These are *public streets*. A camera is never improper anywhere other sets of human eyes might be. The red-light cameras are a mixed bag. Accuracy is an issue, and they may in fact cause some additional accidents as motorists slam on the brakes for fear of running afoul of the technology. Then there is the Sixth Amendment guarantee of confronting the witnesses against us, hard to do when it is a chunk of metal twenty-five feet above the roof of your car.

But all of these measures combined do not rise to the level of Nazi Germany. We can argue all we like about which law enforcement capabilities we wish to restrict and which to advance, but before we haul out the police state label, we would do well to revisit the stories of those who actually lived in one.

Libertarians are not anti-police, but they do blanch at some of the armaments modern cops are deploying these days. And "deploying" might be the apt term in view of the military vibe some police departments are giving off. But when people ask why police need tanks and big guns, I always ask them if they have seen footage from the location of the latest riots. The reason police departments have riot gear is they occasionally have to respond to rioters.

I've always thought potentially violent mobs would have second thoughts if they had a reasonable expectation of meeting heavy weaponry in response. No one advocates injudicious use of these resources, but the logic of the military applies here—the best weapon is the one you do not have to use because troublemakers know it exists.

All of these law enforcement measures require trust. Every one of these technologies and tactics is subject to abuse. If that happens, it's not a hardware problem, it's a people problem. If the public decides it wants to roll back police power, it will do so through legislatures and city councils. Police states happen when authoritarian leaders foist them on the people. American police have been given various tools because we want them to have them.

27

HOPE

Our problems are too big to solve.

If you've read this far, you might have the feeling that we're sunk. It was great while it lasted, this American experiment, but our culture is poisoned, our Constitution is in tatters, our families are fractured, and our nation and the world are just too screwed up.

This is not an uninformed view. There is a basis for believing that the verdict is in, and we are not able to sustain the enterprise we embarked on two and a half centuries ago—a land that would grace the world with a shining example of self-government.

In *The Fate of Empires and the Search for Survival* (1978), Sir John Glubb identified the stages powerful nations supposedly go through: the pioneer phase, the conquest phase, then commerce, affluence, intellect, decadence, and finally decline and collapse. It doesn't take too much imagination to discern this pattern in American history. Evidence of the decadence and decline phases is all around us. Our media-saturated culture celebrates narcissism, self-indulgence, and empty excess; dependency on government is rewarded and growing; kids growing up with a married mom and dad are a rarity; and presidential edicts force schools to open girls' locker rooms to men. So yes, we might be about done here.

But what if enough people choose otherwise? What if we recall the moments in our history when things looked awful and we fought through them? Amid rampant historical illiteracy, it is a tall order to expect wide appreciation of where we have come from. But if we can rekindle interest in the remarkable American journey, maybe we can climb out from cynicism and defeatism and save ourselves.

That sounds pretty dramatic: "save ourselves." Are we really on the brink of extinction? Are things that bad? I'd like to think not. But why not summon all hands on deck, whether we are a decade or a century from turning into a failed state?

Now is the time to exercise a little historical imagination. What was it like to wonder whether we could ever get out from under the British crown? What was it like when Americans were killing Americans in a Civil War that might have broken us into two countries? There are people still alive who remember when Hitler was in the news every day and no one knew if he could be stopped.

My parents were approaching adolescence when America entered World War II. I remember their stories of a country that sacrificed deeply for the war effort and their memories of a unifying spirit across the nation as fathers, sons, and brothers went off to save the lives of people in other lands. I imagined their childhoods, coastal lights dimmed for fear of offshore enemy submarines, food and fuel rationed, no new cars or even tires for sale. Then I remembered my own adolescence, when I could get pretty bummed if the store did not have the particular Hot Wheels car I craved.

We are mightily spoiled. We aren't asked to do without candy bars or cars in wartime today. After 9/11, we were actually introduced to the opposite of sacrifice—the notion that terrorists would win if we did *not* engage in consumer spending. "What did you do for the war effort today, Bill?" "Bought a gas grill, Frank."

Thousands of Americans have given life, limb, blood, and sweat to our current fitful war effort, so it's not as if we have exhausted our capacity to wage what is truly a battle of civilizations. But can we spark a desire to resuscitate our own civilization?

The British Empire could well have crushed our wild ideas of independence. The Civil War could have split our nation into something unrecognizable. The roads to racial justice and women's rights might have been even longer. There are medical miracles that may have gone undiscovered, or footprints never left on the moon. But we dug deep to do good, fight evil, and expand our horizons.

Many of today's problems are self-inflicted wounds. So often we have met the enemy and it is us. But shouldn't the nation that won its independence from the greatest power on earth, fought off global evils, and spread a message of liberty around the world be able to climb out of its current hole?

It may seem that I have offered partisan solutions—just apply enough conservatism and watch things get better. That's not a bad idea, but a real solution goes even farther. Remember when Democrats believed in a strong military and did not recoil at biblical teachings? Remember when liberal leaders would stick up for the police? Remember when people of all political stripes assumed that our nation was great because of a common set of values, a shared language, and strong borders? Is it crazy to think we can have that back?

Between self-absorbed millennials and game-addicted
adolescents, the future is lost.

Here's a scary question: If the Greatest Generation gave us the Baby Boomers, and the Baby Boomers gave us the millennials, what will the millennials give us? As discouraging as the answer may seem, there are glimmers of hope.

As I write this, my son has just turned thirteen. My wife and I allow him limited access to the devices and online pursuits that have sucked the brains and social skills out of countless other kids of many ages. Even the most vigilant households face challenges keeping the kids' faces away from screens.

I was going to say today's parents tell stories of youths spent largely outside, playing with friends, and interacting with the real world, but those yarns may be more likely from today's grandparents. Twenty-first-century dads could well have spent their teen years in the bleaching glow of video games rather than the heart-pumping rhythms of street football.

My grown daughter runs a game and comic book store. I walked away from comic books when I was in junior high school. Many of her customers today are in their thirties and forties. This is not necessarily bad; wide interests can be a part of a fulfilling life. But it's reasonable to worry that too many men are absorbed by interests more suited to boys, while manhood takes a beating at every turn. Where will the next generations of men with broad and useful skills come from—men who exude masculinity, men driven by a strong work ethic, uninterested in spending the first decade of adulthood under their parents' roof?

Today's young women are not as likely to be hunched over Grand Theft Auto in the wee hours, but many share with their millennial brothers that now-familiar sense of entitlement, short attention span, and unrealistic expectations.

If these are the leaders of the 2030s and beyond, we are toast, right?

There are two sources of optimism. First, today's twentysomethings may be entirely different creatures by the time they are in their forties and fifties. Aren't we all? And second, while there is some truth in every stereotype, there are young people all around us who are making their parents proud and their nation and world a better place.

The easy first example is the all-volunteer military we have had for decades. When the draft ended in the mid-seventies, all of our new soldiers, sailors, and Marines were there because they chose to be. That was inspiring well before 9/11. Since then, the grit, devotion, and determination shown by the men and women who have served in our war against terror has earned fitting comparisons with the Greatest Generation of the 1940s. The twenty-three-year-old you meet today may be a spoiled shell of a man withered by self-indulgence, or he may have just returned from dodging IEDs so our nation can be safe.

Data show young adults becoming more secular, but I constantly run across those who are devoted deeply to their faith, sensing added urgency because they see at an early age the societal costs of a nation distancing from God. This is purely anecdotal, and certainly a product of my vantage point in Texas, but everywhere I travel I see and hear of waves of young people doing charity work, even missionary work. As many as in generations past? Maybe not, but they are far from extinct.

Apart from faith, for every undermotivated millennial there may be another who is trying to start a business, or busting butt in school on the way to becoming a doctor, lawyer, or engineer. Hard-working young adults are everywhere. Bernie Sanders rallies may have been filled with kids who could just taste that free college paid for by the evil rich, but some kids are working their own way through college, or delaying or sidestepping it to jump into the real working world.

The coming years will see either a return to an energetic and virtuous young adult culture or a further slide. It's not wholly on them; the best way to see better young adults in the next generation will be to give them better parenting in this one.

Our culture is past saving.

Public opinion is not hurtling leftward on every social issue. On gay marriage and drug legalization it is, and it is hard to see those horses back in the barn any time soon. But for more than a decade, the youngest adults have moved away from years of permissiveness on abortion.[1] This does not mean that eighteen- to twenty-nine-year-olds will change their views on marriage and drug laws, but it shows that it is impossible to know where the river of public opinion will cut its path.

Pessimism is not irrational these days, but pessimists are often pleasantly surprised. Maybe they will see evidence of an improving America in the coming years. Maybe we will start to rediscover the things we have lost: an appreciation of our nation's history and its decency, the priority of families, and a shared American spirit to remedy the problems I've identified here, and maybe a few more that I may have missed.

For a nation of 320 million to get its act together, it must first believe that it can be done. The world is indeed upside down. Climbing out of our current circumstances will require faith, first in the broad sense of the word—confidence that we can succeed. But we would do well to rediscover the faith of our Founders as well, a deep conviction that God's very hand was upon our nation at birth. Believers know he is still in control, even though he does not guarantee that political and social winds will blow in a certain way.

After the death of Moses, Joshua faced enormous challenges in leading the Israelites. God's reassurance to him should echo with us as we figure out how to set things right: "Be strong and courageous. Do not be afraid; do not be discouraged, for the Lord your God will be with you wherever you go." (Joshua 1:9).

American success will depend on cooperation across religious lines, racial lines, and up and down our class structure. We're not going to agree on everything; we won't agree on most things, and that's fine. No one should want to return to the America of the past. We've made too much genuine progress. But many of the trails we have blazed have taken us to dark and dangerous places. When people say they "want their country back," they mean they want to reclaim the foundation of American identity.

Since 1956, our national motto has been "In God we trust," a basic profession of faith. Religious freedom gives us the option under law to follow whatever faith we choose. But our previous motto—*E pluribus unum*—dating back to before the Constitution's ratification, is the one that we need to rediscover. If we can rekindle the sense that we are one land assembled from many peoples and beliefs, maybe our children and grandchildren can hold a view not long ago taken for granted—that through good times and bad, America's future is worth looking forward to.

ACKNOWLEDGMENTS

In any book I am honored to write, my first gratitude goes to God, who truly makes all things possible. He made it possible for my parents to meet, marry, and raise me. He gave me the path to my incomparable wife and two wonderful children. Lisa makes every day a joy, Regina makes me so proud as she works her way through her twenties, and Ethan now leads us with his bright spirit on the adventure into teenagerhood. I love you guys so much, and everything I do is for you.

Professionally, my home is the Salem Media Group, which gives me stability and satisfaction in a radio industry often known for neither. Four years in with the Salem family, and I have come to appreciate even more deeply the vision of its co-founder and CEO, Ed Atsinger, and the California-based team that guides our individual stations, the Salem Radio Network, and the various print and online platforms the company has acquired.

I've worked for a lot of radio companies, usually enjoying complete creative freedom. Salem offers me that in addition to the fulfillment of being on a team with a mission. We have a lot of talk stations, Christian music stations, and faith-based talk stations. I have come to know many of my corporate colleagues at every level, and I am proud to be striving alongside them in pursuit of various earthly and spiritual goals.

One of Salem's acquisitions has been Regnery Publishing, a company kind enough to have worked with me on 2014's *Lone Star America: How Texas Can Save Our Country*. We struck up a relationship before their company joined with mine, and now that we're all kin, it's an even greater pleasure. From the management of Marji Ross and Harry Crocker to the editing friendship I have been fortunate to forge with Tom Spence, I hope to enjoy their companionship for a long time.

I enjoy the constant company of my daily radio family led by the always encouraging General Manager John Peroyea. Producer Ronda Moreland, Technical Director Shane Bell, and News Director Gordon Griffin not only make the show what it is, they make my working world what it is: a delightful and engaging place where I get to sling hot topics not just with listeners but with my friends. I could not be more grateful to share my mornings with them.

In honing a list of things to address in these pages, I've been enlightened and inspired by the hosts of the shows that appear alongside mine on 660 AM The Answer in Dallas–Fort Worth. They include the familiar Salem Radio Network programs hosted by Bill Bennett, Hugh Hewitt, Michael Medved, and Dennis Prager, whom I am now proud to call friends as well as colleagues.

Also in that lineup is Mike Gallagher, whom I have known far longer. We speak often, on and off the air, and I tell him what a gift our relationship is every day. We've been through a lot together, in radio and the real world, and it is a blessing to be his friend.

It is still a delight after twelve years to share my thoughts in the *Dallas Morning News*, as well as at Townhall.com, another outpost in the growing Salem empire. I thank them for letting me rant in column form. Thanks also to the two Dallas–Fort Worth TV stations that allow me to share thoughts on a weekly basis: Fox affiliate KDFW and ABC's WFAA.

On the rotation through a daily radio show and its various offshoots, beginning and ending each day in the happy home I get to share with my family, I can't possibly count all of the friends and co-workers I get the pleasure to share life's path with. We cherish a worship home at Fellowship Church in Grapevine, Texas, under the joyous guidance of Ed and Lisa Young, who provide the constant message that no matter how off-track the nation and the world may get, we are all under God's care and called to be obedient to his plan. It is that clarity that completes the happiness I can bring to every task, large and small.

Writing this book has been a busy road trip through just about everything I talk about on the radio for a living. Distilling it into book form was alternately invigorating and daunting. Man, do we have a lot of work to do!

Thanks for consuming my work. Maybe it will inspire you to devote part of your life to the repairs suggested here. Maybe it just helps kill time on a flight. Either way, I deeply appreciate your time.

NOTES

1: HISTORY

1. Ray Raphael, *Constitutional Myths: What We Get Wrong and How to Get It Right* (New York: The New Press, 2013), 162.

2: GOVERNMENT

1. Michael Muskal, "Texas Police Chief Tells Group What It Can Do with Its Demand to Dump 'In God We Trust' Motto," *Los Angeles Times*, September 30, 2015, http://www.latimes.com/nation/la-na-god-we-trust-fly-kite-childress-chief-20150929-story.html.
2. Robert Rector and Rachel Sheffield, "The War on Poverty after 50 Years," Heritage Foundation Backgrounder #2955, http://www.heritage.org/research/reports/2014/09/the-war-on-poverty-after-50-years.

3. William J. Bennett, "Obama's 'Life of Julia' Is the Wrong Vision for America," CNN, May 9, 2012, http://www.cnn.com/2012/05/09/opinion/bennett-obama-campaign/index.html.

3: ENERGY

1. James MacDougald, *Unsustainable: How Big Government, Taxes and Debt Are Wrecking America* (Marsden House Publishers, 2010), 20.
2. Brian Viner, "Why the World Isn't Running Out of Oil," *Telegraph*, February 19, 2013, http://www.telegraph.co.uk/news/earth/energy/oil/9867659/Why-the-world-isnt-running-out-of-oil.html.
3. President George W. Bush 2006 State of the Union Address, *Washington Post* transcript, http://www.washingtonpost.com/wp-dyn/content/article/2006/01/31/AR2006013101468.html.

4: IMMIGRATION

1. *United States v. Wong Kim Ark*, 169 U.S. 649 (1898), https://supreme.justia.com/cases/federal/us/169/649/#715.
2. Text of floor speech by Senator Jacob Howard, May 23, 1866, http://www.yale.edu/lawweb/jbalkin/conlaw/senatorhowardspeechonthefourteenthamendment.pdf.
3. U.S. Census data, http://www.census.gov/2010census/data/apportionment-pop-text.php.
4. Josh Harkinson, "How H-1B Visas Are Screwing Tech Workers," *Mother Jones*, February 22, 2013, http://www.motherjones.com/politics/2013/02/silicon-valley-h1b-visas-hurt-tech-workers.
5. Julia Preston, "Pink Slips at Disney. But First, Training Foreign Replacements," *New York Times*, June 3, 2015, http://www.nytimes.com/2015/06/04/us/last-task-after-layoff-at-disney-train-foreign-replacements.html?_r=0.

6. Steven A. Camarota, "Welfare Use by Legal and Illegal Immigrant Households," Center for Immigration Studies, September 2015, http://cis.org/Welfare-Use-Legal-Illegal-Immigrant-Households.

5: EDUCATION

1. National Center for Education Statistics, Fast Facts, http://nces.ed.gov/fastfacts/display.asp?id=28.
2. "Estimated Average Annual Salary of Teachers in Public Elementary and Secondary Schools, by State: Selected Years, 1969–70 through 2012–13, National Center for Education Statistics, https://nces.ed.gov/programs/digest/d13/tables/dt13_211.60.asp.
3. J. Michael Smith, "U.S. Department of Education: Homeschooling Continues to Grow," Home School Legal Defense Association, https://www.hslda.org/docs/news/2013/201309030.asp.
4. "Clinton Touts Success of Public Charter Schools," CNN, May 4, 2000, https://www.hslda.org/docs/news/2013/201309030.asp.

6: THE BUSINESS WORLD

1. Excerpt of Milton Friedman on *Donahue*, 1979, https://www.youtube.com/watch?v=RWsx1X8PV_A.
2. C. S. Lewis, "The Humanitarian Theory of Punishment," *God in the Dock: Essays on Theology and Ethics*, Walter Hooper, ed. (Grand Rapids, MI: Eerdmans, 1972), 287–300.
3. *Fortune*'s Global 500 rankings for 2015: http://fortune.com/global500/.
4. Mike Gallagher, *50 Things Liberals Love to Hate* (New York: Simon and Schuster, 2012), 51.

7: HEALTH CARE

1. Sally Pipes, "The Ugly Realities of Socialized Medicine Are Not Going Away," *Forbes*, December 19, 2011, http://www.forbes.com/sites/sallypipes/2011/12/19/the-ugly-realities-of-socialized-medicine-are-not-going-away-3/print/.

2. Denis Campbell, "Care Quality Commission: Two-Thirds of Hospitals Offering Substandard Care," *Guardian*, October 15, 1015, http://www.theguardian.com/society/2015/oct/15/two-thirds-hospitals-substandard-care-care-quality-commission.

3. Melissa Scott, "Healthy in Cuba, Sick in America?," ABC News, September 2, 2007, http://abcnews.go.com/Exclusiva/story?id=3568278&page=1.

4. Philip Klein, "Obamacare's Big Question Mark," *Washington Examiner*, June 4, 2015, http://www.washingtonexaminer.com/obamacares-big-question-mark/article/2565614.

5. Merrill Matthews, "My Wife's Losing Her Obamacare Coverage because the Insurer Lost $400 Million," *Forbes*, August 3, 2015, http://www.forbes.com/sites/merrillmatthews/2015/08/03/my-wifes-losing-her-obamacare-coverage-because-the-insurer-lost-400-million/.

6. Diana Furchtgott-Roth and Jared Meyer, *Disinherited: How Washington Is Betraying America's Young* (New York: Encounter Books, 2015); see also Furchtgott-Roth and Meyer, "Obamacare Is a Horror Story for Young Americans," National Review Online, May 19, 2015, http://www.nationalreview.com/article/418322/obamacare-horror-story-young-americans.

8: LIFE

1. Pam Belluck, "Pregnancy Centers Gain Influence in Anti-Abortion Arena," *New York Times*, January 4, 2013, http://www.nytimes.com/2013/01/05/health/pregnancy-centers-gain-influence-in-anti-abortion-fight.html?_r=1&pagewanted=all.

2. Rich Lowry, "Planned Parenthood's Pathetic '3 percent' lie," *New York Post*, August 3, 2015, available online at: http://nypost.com/2015/08/03/planned-parenthoods-pathetic-3-percent-lie/.

9: HATE

1. Glenn Kessler, "The 'Equal Pay Day' Factoid That Women Make 78 Cents for Every Dollar Earned by Men," *Washington Post*, April 2, 2015, https://www.washingtonpost.com/news/fact-checker/wp/2015/04/02/the-equal-pay-day-factoid-that-women-make-78-cents-for-every-dollar-earned-by-men/.

2. "Voters See 'War On Women' as Politics, not Reality," *Rasmussen Reports*, September 28, 2014, http://www.rasmussenreports.com/public_content/politics/general_politics/september_2014/voters_see_war_on_women_as_politics_not_reality.

10: RELIGION

1. Remarks by President George W. Bush, September 17, 2001, released by the White House, http://georgewbush-whitehouse.archives.gov/news/releases/2001/09/20010917-11.html.

2. "Where Terrorism Finds Support in the Muslim World," Pew Research Center, May 23, 2008, http://www.pewglobal.org/2006/05/23/where-terrorism-finds-support-in-the-muslim-world/.

3. Igor Bobic, "John Kasich Tells Critics of Medicaid Expansion to Read the Bible," Huffington Post, October 6, 2015, http://www.huffingtonpost.com/entry/john-kasich-bible-medicaid_56140a54e4b022a4ce5fb1e3.

4. Joe Hallett and Catherine Candisky, "Kasich Makes Faith Argument for Medicaid," *Columbus Dispatch*, June 19, 2013, http://www.dispatch.com/content/stories/local/2013/06/18/kasich-will-never-give-up-fight-to-expand-medicaid.html.

5. Russell Kirk, *The Conservative Mind: From Burke to Eliot*, seventh revised edition (Washington: Regnery Publishing, 1985), 8.

11: HUMAN NATURE

1. G. K. Chesterton, *Orthodoxy*, in *The Collected Works of G. K. Chesterton*, vol. I, David Dooley, ed. (San Francisco: Ignatius Press, 1986), 216.
2. D'Vera Cohn, Gretchen Livingston and Wendy Wang, "After Decades of Decline, a Rise in Stay-at-Home Mothers," Pew Research Center, April 8, 2014, http://www.pewsocialtrends.org/2014/04/08/after-decades-of-decline-a-rise-in-stay-at-home-mothers/.
3. Gretchen Livingston, "Growing Number of Dads Home with the Kids," Pew Research Center, June 5, 2014, http://www.pewsocialtrends.org/2014/06/05/growing-number-of-dads-home-with-the-kids/.

12: FIGHTING TERROR

1. FBI, Hate Crime Statistics 2014, https://www.fbi.gov/about-us/cjis/ucr/hate-crime/2014/topic-pages/incidentsandoffenses_final.
2. "Northern Virginiastan," *Investor's Business Daily* editorial, February 26, 2007, http://news.investors.com/022607-495105-northern-virginiastan.htm?p=full.
3. Julie Hirschfeld Davis, "It's Either Iran Deal or 'Some Form of War,' Obama Warns," *New York Times,* August 5, 2015, http://www.nytimes.com/2015/08/06/us/politics/obama-urges-critics-of-iran-deal-to-ignore-drumbeat-of-war.html?_r=2.

13: MARRIAGE

1. Charles Lane, "Colorado's Marijuana Experiment Has a Bitter Aftertaste," *Washington Post*, October 23, 2014, https://www.washingtonpost.com/

opinions/charles-lane-colorados-marijuana-experiment-has-a-bitter-after taste/2014/10/23/3fb7b34c-5a2d-11e4-bd61-346aee66ba29_story.html.

15: THE ECONOMY

1. "Share of Adults Living in Middle-Income Households Is Falling," Pew Research Center, December 8, 2015, http://www.pewsocialtrends. org/2015/12/09/the-american-middle-class-is-losing-ground/st_2015-12-09_middle-class-03/.

2. Tami Luhby, "Middle Class No Longer Dominates in the U.S.," CNN Money, December 9, 2015, http://money.cnn.com/2015/12/09/news/ economy/middle-class/.

3. "Top 10 Percent of Earners Paid 68 Percent of Federal Income Taxes," "Federal Budget in Pictures," Heritage Foundation, http://www.heritage. org/federalbudget/top10-percent-income-earners.

4. Chris Edwards and Daniel J. Murphy, "Employment Training Programs: Ineffective and Unneeded," downsizinggovernment.org, June 2011, http:// www.downsizinggovernment.org/labor/employment-training-programs#_ ednref17.

5. Tim Worstall, "Checking Seattle's Minimum Wage: Look, There Are the Job Losses," *Forbes*, October 23, 2015, http://www.forbes.com/sites/ timworstall/2015/10/23/checking-seattles-15-minimum-wage-look-theres-the-job-losses/#a1e9c765da40.

6. Lydia dePillis, "Minimum-Wage Offensive Could Speed Arrival of Robot-Powered Restaurants," *Washington Post*, August 15, 2015, https://www. washingtonpost.com/business/capitalbusiness/minimum-wage-offensive-could-speed-arrival-of-robot-powered-restaurants/2015/08/16/35f284ea-3f6f-11e5-8d45-d815146f81fa_story.html.

16: THE WORLD

1. Nicholas Eberstadt, "Five Myths about the World's Population," *Washington Post*, November 4, 2011, https://www.washingtonpost.com/opinions/five-myths-about-the-worlds-population/2011/10/26/gIQArjSWmM_story.html.
2. "World Population to Peak by 2055: Report," September 9, 2013, CNBC.com, http://www.cnbc.com/id/101018722.
3. Elise Labbott, "John Kerry: Some Sanctions Relief Money for Iran Will Go to Terrorism," CNN, January 21, 2016, http://www.cnn.com/2016/01/21/politics/john-kerry-money-iran-sanctions-terrorism/.

17: CRIME AND PUNISHMENT

1. "Arrest-Related Deaths, 2003–2009—Statistical Tables," Bureau of Justice Statistics, http://www.bjs.gov/index.cfm?ty=pbdetail&iid=2228.
2. Kimberly Kindy, Marc Fisher, Julie Tate, and Jennifer Jenkins, "A Year of Reckoning: Police Fatally Shoot Nearly 1,000," *Washington Post*, December 26, 2015, http://www.washingtonpost.com/sf/investigative/2015/12/26/a-year-of-reckoning-police-fatally-shoot-nearly-1000/.
3. Deroy Murdock, "Black Lives Matters Numbers Are Bogus," *New York Post*, November 6, 2015, http://nypost.com/2015/11/06/black-lives-matters-numbers-are-bogus/.
4. Barry Latzer, "The Myth of Mass Incarceration," *Wall Street Journal*, February 22, 2016, http://www.wsj.com/articles/the-myth-of-mass-incarceration-1456184736.

18: GUNS

1. Michael Planty, Ph.D., and Jennifer Truman, Ph.D., "Firearm Violence, 1993–2011," Bureau of Justice Statistics, May 7, 2013, http://www.bjs.gov/index.cfm?ty=pbdetail&iid=4616.

2. D'Vera Cohn, Paul Taylor, Mark Hugo Lopez, Catherine Gallagher, Kim Parker, and Kevin Maass, "Gun Homicide Rate Down 49% since 1993 Peak; Public Unaware," Pew Research Center, http://www.pewsocialtrends. org/2013/05/07/gun-homicide-rate-down-49-since-1993-peak-public-unaware/.

3. Larry Bell, "Disarming Realities: As Gun Sales Soar, Gun Crimes Plummet," *Forbes*, May 14, 2013, http://www.forbes.com/sites/ larrybell/2013/05/14/disarming-realities-as-gun-sales-soar-gun-crimes-plummet/#e8a04ca7de9e.

4. Crime Prevention Research Center, "Concealed Carry Permit Holders across the United States," July 9, 2014, http://crimeresearch.org/wp-content/ uploads/2014/07/Concealed-Carry-Permit-Holders-Across-the-United-States.pdf.

19: DRUGS

1. Seth Motel, "6 Facts about Marijuana," Pew Research Center, April 14, 2015, http://www.pewresearch.org/fact-tank/2015/04/14/6-facts-about-marijuana/.

2. Linda Chavez, "Rocky Mountain High," creators.com, December 27, 2013, https://www.creators.com/read/linda-chavez/12/13/rocky-mountain-high.

3. Jack Healy, "After 5 Months of Sales, Colorado Sees the Downside of a Legal High," *New York Times*, May 31, 2014, http://www.nytimes. com/2014/06/01/us/after-5-months-of-sales-colorado-sees-the-downside-of-a-legal-high.html?_r=0.

20: CLIMATE

1. Patrick J., Michaels, *Meltdown: The Predictable Distortion of Global Warming by Scientists, Politicians and the Media* (Washington, DC: Cato Institute, 2004), 115.

2. Jaclyn Schiff, "Al Gore Does Sundance," Associated Press, January 26, 2006, http://www.cbsnews.com/news/2006-al-gore-does-sundance/.

3. "U.N. Official Reveals Real Reason Behind Warming Scare," *Investor's Business Daily* editorial, February 10, 2015, http://www.investors.com/politics/editorials/climate-change-scare-tool-to-destroy-capitalism/.

21: DEFENDING OUR NATION

1. "Women in Land Combat, Selected Findings—1992 Presidential Commission," Center for Military Readiness, November 18, 2004, http://www.cmrlink.org/content/women-in-combat/34414/women_in_land_combat?year=2004.

2. Aaron Belkin and Melissa Levitt, "Homosexuality and the Israel Defense Forces: Did Lifting the Gay Ban Undermine Military Performance?," *Armed Forces and Society*, Vol. 27, No.4, Summer 2001, 549, http://www.palmcenter.org/files/Homsexuality%20and%20Israel%20Defense%20Forces_0.pdf.

3. Gregory Newbold, "What Tempers the Steel of an Infantry Unit," War on the Rocks, September 9, 2015, http://warontherocks.com/2015/09/what-tempers-the-steel-of-an-infantry-unit/.

22: THE SUPREME COURT

1. "Remarks by the President Announcing Judge Merrick Garland as His Nominee to the Supreme Court," White House Press Release, March 16, 2016, https://www.whitehouse.gov/the-press-office/2016/03/16/remarks-president-announcing-judge-merrick-garland-his-nominee-supreme.

23: THE OBAMA ERA

1. Transcript of Jimmy Carter's speech, "Crisis of Confidence," July 15, 1979, PBS, http://www.pbs.org/wgbh/americanexperience/features/primary-resources/carter-crisis/.
2. Aaron Blake, "African Americans See Less Harmony with Police—and Also with Whites," *Washington Post*, August 26, 2014, https://www.washingtonpost.com/news/the-fix/wp/2014/08/26/poll-african-americans-see-less-harmony-with-police-and-also-with-whites/.

24: CONSERVATISM

1. Mark Berman and Kevin Sullivan, "The Oregon Standoff and the Recent History of Anti-Government Groups in the U.S.," *Washington Post*, January 4, 2016, https://www.washingtonpost.com/news/post-nation/wp/2016/01/04/the-oregon-standoff-and-the-recent-history-of-anti-government-groups-in-the-u-s/.
2. Karen Pierog, "Republicans Gain Big in State Legislative Elections," Reuters, November 5, 2014, http://www.reuters.com/article/us-usa-elections-states-idUSKBN0IP2HB20141105.
3. Laura Saunders, "Top 20% of Earners Pay 84% of Income Tax," *Wall Street Journal*, April 10, 2015, http://www.wsj.com/articles/top-20-of-earners-pay-84-of-income-tax-1428674384.
4. "Pro-Administration War Rally," C-SPAN, February 3, 1991, http://www.c-span.org/video/?16166-1/proadministration-war-rally.

25: LIBERALISM

1. Henry Olsen, "What Voters Want: A Prez Who Cares," *New York Post*, November 9, 2012, http://nypost.com/2012/11/09/what-voters-want-a-prez-who-cares/.

2. Debbie Georgatos, *Ladies, Can We Talk? America Needs Our Vote* (Dallas: CWT Publications, 2012), 15.

3. Kyle Kondik and Jeffrey Skelly, "Mind the Gap," *Sabato's Crystal Ball*, University of Virginia Center for Politics, September 12, 2013, http://www.centerforpolitics.org/crystalball/articles/mind-the-gap/.

27: HOPE

1. "Generational Differences on Abortion Narrow," gallup.com, March 12, 2010, http://www.gallup.com/poll/126581/generational-differences-abortion-narrow.aspx.

INDEX